BARE BEAUTY

To Shannon

In love and Oneness
and so much gratitude
for the Bare Beauty
that is You!

[signature]

BARE BEAUTY

my journey of AWAKENING

BEKI

crowell

Book cover desgn by Tamra Scott
Cover and interior Artwork by Beki
Back cover photo by Joanna Crowell
Book interior design by Sherman Evans

Published 2018
in the United States of America

ISBN 978-1-7326566-0-4

SOULART

To Chaz, the son who delivered me to the threshold of my pain,
pushing me beyond all known limitations
so that I may give birth to the fearless, flagrantly free-spirited-One.
that is both you and me.
To my other two gurus,
Noah and Kai who soothe and stretch me with their own unique Beauty.
To the many midwives seen and unseen who have companioned me
through my many labors
that Awaken me again and again to the
Bare Beauty in All that Is.

Bare Beauty

I ache to see the unseen
To breathe in the scent of
Love
shared.
I want to touch the
beauty of your
bare naked
Soul
that radiates
from INSIDE
the deepest, widest part
of my being.
I thirst for the color of sensuous rivers,
drinking in the Divine nectar
of Mother Earth

I lie open, bare, empty,
waiting patiently,
peacefully,
with gentle anticipation,
to be penetrated,
Filled
with beauty,
My beauty,
Your beauty,
Inner,
Outer,
Empty,
Bare Beauty

I close my eyes,
as my heart awakens,
vibrating with color,
light,
sound,
seeping sweet, syrupy
warmth
into my veins,
watering the plants of my Garden of Eden,
Awakening me
Gently, prodding me
to open my eyes
to see
The Bare Beauty of
all things
seen and unseen.

CONTENTS

Paintings by Beki

Bare Beauty

1

INTRODUCTION
Fearless
Fleeting Fearlessness

O N A NEW YEAR'S DAY a few years ago, I said to a friend, "I feel fearless." My alignment with joy and peace and freedom felt so strong that the feeling of fearlessness was palpable enough for me to speak it out loud, to claim it.

I am quite certain that fearlessness is not an ordinary proclamation for me. As a matter of fact, I have lived most of my life feeling a low level of fear. An imperceptible hum, like my HVAC system, that I am barely aware of until it shuts off and there is a brief moment of relief—quiet, peaceful relief from the ongoing static of artificial sound.

Fear has been like that for me. Mostly it has been bearable and almost inaudible. Then, occasionally it spikes into a crescendo of downright terror. In those moments, I am no longer in control. I flail helplessly for minutes, hours, days and sometimes I am consumed by this unbearable state of disconnection for months. Once, well twice, I experienced an entire year of feeling disconnected after giving birth to my first and then again with my second son. Postpartum depression, they call it. For one whole year, both times, I rode the choppy waves of fear, depression, anxiety, panic and guilt. At the same time, my heart was being torn open with a love that terrified me. My love for my babies was so fierce and consuming that the guilt I felt for all the other crazy and uncontrollable feelings was at times unbearable. Yet, I made it through, without even knowing that I was in a hormonal hurricane.

Both times after the first year of mothering came to an end, I was propelled into an irrefutable Awakening. Still, Fearlessness eluded me. Yet, a sweet awareness of my Divine nature trickled over and through me, and a knowing and peace seeped into my experience that has never left me.

Awakening occurs in us gradually and steadily, and once it begins, there is no going back. There is only a propelling movement forward. This propulsion contains within it a contraction that allows for this continued motion to occur. It allows for the *expansion* to happen. We came forth in this physical, human experience for the pure joy of EXPANSION. At times, the contraction is perceived as moving backward, sliding back into the unconsciousness of pre-awakening. Yet, I see the contraction as the necessary movement to propel us forward on our journey of Awakening, our eternal path of expansion! It is essential for the birth and manifestation of ALL that is. As the human baby requires the natural contractions of its mother's womb to propel it into this physical world, we all need to experience contrasting conditions to open us up

2

to the awareness of what we truly desire. Our awareness of what we don't want (the contraction) gives birth to the desire of what we do want. The result is expansion. I have come to understand that this expansion is not only in our own lives, but also our collective 'labor and birth' is indeed the prolusion that allows for the expansion of the whole universe!

What makes the process so intolerable at times is the human propensity to become fixated on the condition that gave rise to the expansive desire. Resistance is introduced, and we get stuck in the birth canal. The contraction is not able to do its work of propelling life forward. As with childbirth, if the mother is resistant—fearful, clenching, fighting the process—the labor will be more painful and drawn-out, and the fruition of the labor is delayed. And yet, the baby must be born regardless of our resistance. Eventually, we are worn down enough to *allow* the manifestation to be realized. Life will win out in the end. Expansion is inevitable.

Of course, this analogy is not perfect. Sometimes, yet rarely in the whole scheme of things, a baby is born without breath, or it is not what we expected or thought we desired. We then become entangled in another ongoing labor of living in a life with conditions we have no control over that simply seems impossible to bear. However, this is yet another contraction in the stage of Life, which breaks us through into unchartered lands that may bring forth the most glorious expansion of all. It is always our resistance to what is that prolongs the labor, the pain, and at times, downright anguish. When we practice the profound Art of Allowing, then we begin to live our lives more and more unconditionally.

It is now my spiritual practice to live my life Unconditionally. Unconditional Love means being aligned with the love that I am, within and in spite of any condition, wanted or unwanted.

Within a short period of beginning this mindful practice of Unconditional Love, I sat with this friend on New Year's Day and shared my new sense of freedom that felt like Fearlessness.

The labor has been long and glorious. I can honestly say that I give thanks for each and every contraction that brings me to this continuous never-ending, eternal expansion, birthing life over and over and over. . . .

2

Awakening

I MUST HAVE STILL BEEN CRAWLING, because I remember the beautiful, patterned terrain of Oriental and Persian rugs, tall wooden legs of tables and built-in mirrors on doors. While navigating this new world of wonder, I had a profound thought. I contemplated whether or not all of this that surrounded me would still exist if I were not there. That was it. I remember pondering that thought, as a new arrival to this physical reality, in a way that I would now contemplate the mysteries of life. Of course, as we grow up, we all know that this world would continue on after we leave it on a physical level. And yet, as I have evolved and continued the contemplation of my spiritual relationship with life and what is true for me, I have come to believe that I am the creator of my reality and that my reality reflects my perception and my focus. So if I were not here, would the physical world, as I perceive it, be the same? Does it even really matter?

What does matter to me is the awareness that I am the creator of my own reality. I was nineteen or twenty years old when that concept became more of a living truth for me. As a teenager, I had a sense of it and was very much drawn to matters of the spirit and that which went beyond what we see. I knew there was something more, and I explored with curiosity and intrigue, possibilities and accounts of life after death, extrasensory perception, world religions, yoga and channeling of non-physical entities. When I was sixteen, I attended the University of Windsor in Canada, where my father taught Social Ethics in the Religious Studies Department. Although I was an art major, many of the classes I selected were in his department, where I was able to explore the many faces of God.

My Awakening began as soon as I could crawl and this unending expansion has never ceased, although my awareness has ebbed and flowed. So what do I mean when I speak of Awakening? For me, it is the awakening to my True Self, my Divine Nature, my connection and felt Oneness with Source Energy/God. Awakening is a process of becoming aware of what I am and who I really am. The feeling of this awareness is joy, peace, love, freedom, expansiveness. When these pure feelings arise within me, I am filled with deep, sweet gratitude. Bliss, right here, right now . . . Heaven on Earth.

When I was twenty, I began to practice this revelatory awareness: that I created my own reality. It was more than a spiritual concept. I became aware of how my focus on the behavior of others was causing me pain, and when I withdrew my focus and chose a different thought, I felt freer, happier and noticed that the condition that caused the suffering shifted, changed or no longer had power over me. So, my reality was essentially my experience. Reality is similar to perception. It is subjective. It is my perception that is defining my experience and thus, reality.

Later I came to understand that this is the basic idea of the Universal Law of Attraction: what I focus on is what I get, wanted or unwanted. This awareness was so exciting to me. I felt great relief that I was not a victim of life and the happenings around me, but that in truth, I was a powerful co-creator of my life experiences. To some, this responsibility may seem daunting and maybe even disconcerting. For me, it felt true, right and downright liberating!

And yet, my journey at times has been arduous. The human ego would have its way and unconsciousness would sweep over me like a dark grey cloud encompassing a clear blue sky. This is when I could not feel my connection to God. I felt alone, afraid and often desperate. These were times of contraction, and while I may have been feeling miserable, I was being propelled forward, evolving and awakening to my True Divine Self and the expanded version of me.

As I have grown in awareness during this process of Awakening, the contractions are less painful. I am not losing consciousness entirely or for very long. I have gathered tools of inspiration along the path, which have made the journey less arduous and more joyous. Mostly, I understand that the contractions or contrasting conditions are purposeful and necessary to bring forth the birth of my expanded desires.

As a result, my resistance to such unwanted conditions has lessened dramatically. There are even times that I become excited by the opportunity that the contrast offers. When the resistance within me is less, then the expansion within me is more rapid and pleasurable. I dwell less and less in the painful conditions. I see them for what they are. This requires a certain amount of AWAKENED consciousness.

There are many paths to Awakening and the freedom it elicits. This is the story of mine. . . .

3

Into the Unknown

I LIVED IN WINDSOR, ONTARIO, IN Canada from ages two to thirteen. When I graduated from eighth grade and was transitioning into high school, I decided to go live with my mother, and older sister Sarah, who had moved to Nassau, Bahamas. My free-spirited mother had moved there a year before. She applied for a job teaching art at a high school after she saw an ad in her Bahamian roommate's newspaper for the job opening. I was devastated when she told me they were going. I stayed with my father after my parents divorced when I was seven. Although I did not live with my mother and sister, I was able to see them on weekends by taking a two-hour train ride north to London, Ontario. Now they would be way too far away to stay in touch. Even phone calls would be too expensive.

However, it ended up being the best thing that could have happened to me, because my choice to move there to be with them for high school changed my life, and became the catalyst to opening my heart and my creative spirit. I had built up a wall of protection, anger and possibly adolescent angst while living in Windsor. I felt disconnected from my own feelings of love and tenderness.

The reasons could be a combination of factors: divorce, challenging family dynamics with a new stepmother, feeling disconnected from my mother, being biracial in a white world where I did not feel beautiful, a rather intense and serious disposition, normal confusion and growing pains of a pubescent child. I don't feel the reason is so important at this time. Whatever the reason for the contraction, I was primed for a strong and significant propulsion forward. The contraction, as a result of these conditions, along with my lack of awareness of my True Self, were so oppressive that I could not stay in my uncomfortable comfort zone any longer. Expansion was inevitable.

It was the first courageous choice I ever made, moving away from my familiar life: my house, my family, my friends. By then I had three younger siblings, my one-year-old baby sister, Mary Beth, my brother, Daniel, and sister, Joanna. Mostly I felt a loyalty to my father, who was always mild-natured and nurturing. Yet, my discomfort was so intense, along with my desire to be with my mother and Sarah, that I was willing to leave the safety of my known world and take the plunge into a world that was foreign and strange, and so very far away.

Now you may be thinking, "What is so intimidating about going to live with your mother and sister on a beautiful warm tropical island?" It does seem somewhat absurd to think about it now, but then, I was terrified. I was not big on change, and

I was rather shy. It was a world of brown people, like me, and yet that scared me too. They seemed bolder, more colorful and they spoke louder and with an accent that I did not always understand at first. It was a black country. The prime minister was black, the police officers were black, the school I attended was all black, with a majority of black teachers from all over the Caribbean. I used to refer to the faculty as the 'United Nations,' with teachers from Trinidad, Jamaica, France, England, Zimbabwe, Canada and the Bahamas, of course.

My previous school in Canada lacked diversity, to say the least, with a handful of black children or other-than-white children and all white Canadian teachers. It was not the best thing for my self-esteem. My mother is black and father is white. Four of the five children in our family are biracial, and my youngest sister, born of my stepmother and father, is white.

Although my skin color fit into this brown sea of Bahamian humanity, the blackness of the people and brightness of the land was overwhelming and a culture shock. It was unfamiliar terrain, but at the same time, my Soul breathed a deep sigh of relief. She knew she was home. The wet heat wrapped itself around me and swayed my rigid body into a sweet embrace, and within a few weeks my heart began to thaw out . . . its red, hot blood began beating to a new rhythm.

4

Home of my Art

I ALWAYS SAY THAT NASSAU IS the home of my art. It is where my creative spirit woke up. It is not that I did not express myself through art before moving there at the age of thirteen. I was always drawn to art and was pretty good at it. My mother, being an artist, had strong ideas about creativity and not stifling it with coloring books and 'silly' craft activities. She encouraged free expression, without rules. She was a good art teacher for me, as a child and a teenager, because deep within herself, she sensed the need for unleashing creativity from a core place of connection to our Divine Self. Those were not her words, but the awareness was simmering beneath the surface and did not fully become realized until later on.

While in Nassau, I was immersed in a world of art and

artists. My mother and her friends were the hub of my exposure to artistic self-expression and philisophical discourse. We lived in a small two-bedroom apartment. I shared a room with my sister Sarah, furnished with two twin size beds, two small wardrobes for our clothes and a desk for us to share. Our room was divided from the living room with a sliding bamboo screen. The doorway to the apartment was in the kitchen next to the living room, where we had a small table that sat three, possibly four people with a squeeze. We had a pool in the courtyard of the complex and a laundry room next to the pool. It was simple and beautiful. The walls were covered with my mother's artwork, and it was always neat and clean. Even though it was a far cry from my beloved three-story childhood home, it was a small sanctuary of beauty and creativity. In some ways, I felt richer than I ever had. My heart was opening, my art was emerging, I lived in warmth, and there was beauty everywhere you looked. I lived with my mother and sister whom I had deeply missed since my parents' divorce.

My mom situated her easel in the prime location in front of the sliding glass doors in the living room of the second-floor apartment that opened onto a small balcony overlooking the parking lot. I suppose there weren't many choices as to the location of this shared art studio, but it impressed me that the creating of art took precedence in our space. I loved that. It made me aware of the significance of art in our life. I began painting using pictures as a reference, while in high school, developing the skill of painting what I saw. I was not completely realistic in my approach, exercising some creative license, but not much. I wanted the approval of others, and this realistic style felt safe and effective in achieving this unconscious goal. When my mother requested that I paint something without using a reference one quiet Saturday afternoon, after completing our weekly chores, I was surprised by my reaction. I started to cry and emphatically resisted her request. That was when I first became aware that my motive for painting and drawing was connected to my desire to please others, get their approval and to be seen as special and talented. It felt completely unsafe for me to venture out into a world of my own creation. I certainly had many examples around me of artists creating work that went way beyond the rules of realism. Although my mother was more of a realist and specialized in portraits, I always felt she valued the less traditional approach to art. Even though she was my high school art teacher, I still resisted leaving my safe world of art that I thought people would understand and respect.

It was not until I left Nassau and was visiting my mother in Ohio, while I was attending the University of Windsor, that she encouraged me again to paint from 'nothing,' with no reference to copy from. This time she took a different approach, offering that I paint purely for the process, not the end product. As a matter of fact, I would not need to show it to her or anyone at all. She gave me a Walkman cassette player and earphones and left the apartment.

I took the plunge and something magical happened. Spirit took over. I felt free and alive. The image that arose from the white canvas was the essence of me; my face made up of swirling colors of orange, red, turquoise, black, blue, yellow. It was primal and alive, free and fearless. I named her 'Silent Scream' because her/my mouth was open, and yet it was not a scream of anguish, but seemed more like a scream of ecstasy. It really could be renamed 'Awakening', because this was the moment that the artist in me was truly born... Awakened. From this point on, my need for my art to garner approval from others simply dissolved. I had found a direct line to my True Self, my Divine Self, Source Energy. It was so powerful and exhilarating that I never wanted to paint the other way again.

The process of my art moving from the comfortable approach of painting what I saw or observed to the liberating and exhilarating process-oriented approach of creating art from within is the perfect metaphor for the difference between observing our reality and creating our reality. In both cases, we are still creating our reality by our focus. The difference is vast, however, in that when I create from observing what is, then I am experiencing a reality that is an accumulation of everyone else's conscious and unconscious creations. When I create from within, then I am truly being creative. I am molding the clay of my life from the nonphysical, mysterious energy of infinite possibility. I am tapping into my Inner Being, my Soul that is One with God.

As I delved into this luscious realm of unlimited expression, much of what began to emerge from within onto my canvas was definitely a reflection of my years in Nassau. I painted with bold, vibrant primary colors. You could see the dark brown faces of the people, the rich turquoise tones of the Bahamian seas, the yellows and oranges of the Junkanoo Festival. The Afro-Caribbean pulse beat through my paintings, and yet there were no rules. I painted faces with every color in the rainbow and abandoned realism for a freer approach to anatomy and imagery.

While my art was bold and dramatic, daring and provocative, I was happier being in the background, having a more quiet and reserved nature. Yet my art was a reflection of my Inner Being that, of course, was fearless and uninhibited. When I painted then, and still now, I surrendered to this powerful force and allowed the Energy to paint through me. I came to realize that the more I got out of the way, the more satisfied I was with the process and the result. I think of it now as plugging into my Divine Source, when I sit down to the canvas. I meditate before I begin and sometimes throughout the process. If I become too controlling while painting, I step away and come back when I am clearer. The clarity that I attempt to access is that which allows the creation to emerge and to tap into the creative energy that is aligned with the whole of me. I seek the clarity that gives me access to a self-expression that transcends the more limited perception of my human self. The creative process has become a powerful tool for me to merge with my Inner Being and experience the energy of the Awakened Self.

My style has continued to evolve, change and reflect the many facets of my inner and outer life: pregnancy, birth, feminine sensuality, the connection between the human body and nature, the essence of flowers, faces of spirit, ethereal images, the inner landscapes of humanity. The cultural influences became less obvious as my spiritual life and deep yearning to connect with my Source consumed my artistic expression. The truth is, as I create, I am not controlling any of the outcomes. I am allowing it. I am not choosing the content of the artwork; I only define it as it reveals itself to me. The process of painting has been a profound spiritual practice for me and has cultivated my awareness of Divine Energy and how it feels and moves through my life.

My art has been an integral part of my spiritual unfolding and Awakening. It is an expression of pure divine beauty. I am blessed to be surrounded by the beauty of God's Love living in these paintings, and I am grateful to have shared this love with many others over the years.

5

YOGA and GOD

MY FIRST EXPERIENCE WITH YOGA was when I was in University in 1983 and I took a class with Dr. Mehta on the practice and theory of yoga. I was interested in learning about the origins of Yoga and the steps to enlightenment. I don't remember much of the information now. However, I do remember being intrigued by the step that spoke of non-attachment. It would become a touchstone for my spiritual path much later in my life. While it piqued my interest, I resisted the concept and felt it was completely unromantic and the antithesis of what I desired in my human relationships. My perception evolved with the living of life and experiencing the nuances and intensity of navigating the many relationships in my life.

I liked to learn about the asanas (postures), the breathing

techniques and the yogic practices of austerity. I remember Dr. Mehta showing us how to use the neti pot for the purpose of clearing one's nasal passages. It was an anomaly back then, and now that yoga has spread like wildfire through the West, these practices are much more common. It was all so interesting to me then. Dr. Mehta introduced me to a practice that would weave its way through my life for years to come.

While I was attending the University of Windsor and living back in my childhood home, my father invited a man to stay with us. He was a theologian and author and was in town as a guest speaker at the University. He would get up every morning and do yoga in the guest room. He left the door partly open, so as I passed by to use the bathroom, I noticed him doing these postures. My interest and Inner Being were aroused. He was modeling for me the daily practice of yoga. It was all so new to me, and yet I felt a resonance that settled into my bones.

My art professors had indicated a need for me to tone down my colors when I shared with them the paintings that I did outside of class. I still had not had the opportunity to take a painting class, as I was still doing the required prerequisite classes: still-life drawing, life drawing, color fundamentals, art history. It was all rather un-stimulating, to say the least. I was more excited about the classes I was taking in the Religious Studies Department than in my own major in of Fine Arts. All I wanted to do was paint. So, as I was nearing the end of my third semester, in November 1984, I decided to go out and 'live my art, instead of study it'. My sister Sarah had already made the bold choice to leave the University, moving to Boston, Massachusetts, to pursue her desire to dance professionally. She had left that summer and had already begun to navigate the world of dance in Cambridge, where she was taking dance classes and waitressing. I was emboldened by her move and excitedly joined her in Boston. Together, along with another dancer, we found an apartment in North Cambridge to begin our new life of art and independence.

Sarah danced with a couple of prominent modern dance companies in the Boston area and blossomed as a powerful, sensuous, gifted dancer. I found a job in Harvard Square at a small boutique and painted on my days off. While Sarah was immersed in a community of extroverted, exuberant young dancers expressing and creating together, I created in solitude. At eighteen, I struggled to find my place in this big, cold city. I often felt lonely, and at times, depressed by the endless winter.

Eventually, I got a job at the Harriet Tubman House in the South End, where I taught art to children after school and was asked to participate in some art exhibitions. The woman who hired me, Guadulesa, was an artist and had a strong connection to her own spiritual guidance. She exposed me to a world of metaphysical spirituality that was fascinating. I was drawn to the idea of spirit channeling, past lives, worlds and universes beyond this one, life between lives. It opened me up to a dimension that gave me a sense of connection to the Divine Mystery that I always sensed, but had no words to describe adequately. 'God' was a concept that I understood through the lens of religion, passed on to me through my family and societal concepts. I did have my own personal relationship with God that felt intimate and real. I prayed and spoke to God, feeling a certainty of this Divine presence that did not necessarily fit within the walls of churches but lived in my heart. My perception of God certainly was cultivated by the philosophical conversations about life, God, purpose, art, and relationships that were a part of my interaction with my mother and her friends.

I remember reading Shirley MacLaine's book *Out on a Limb* as a teenager and being really lit up by the tale of her experiences regarding her spiritual openings and metaphysical adventures and epiphanies. It was this same book that opened up my mother and that led us on a similar path of spiritual introspection. This metaphysical perspective of God and spirituality felt more natural to me than the more religious one. Although my father was an ordained minister, he was more of an intellectual theologian, and his perspective of God and Christianity seemed to find its expression in his devotion to social justice for the betterment of human life on earth here and now. His spiritual practice was and is social activism.

My stepmother was a Catholic nun for twelve years. When she married my dad, we went to both her Catholic church and Dad's Anglican church alternately. I did not feel much connection to either one. At age twelve or thirteen, I declared that I was an atheist and later claimed I was agnostic for a while. The truth is I did not know what either one of those terms really meant. I just knew that I did not quite resonate with the Christian perspective and did not want to continue going. My parents insisted on my participation, because they felt it would influence the younger siblings to resist going as well. I did believe in God and felt God mostly when I talked and prayed at night. I just did not feel God in church. I guess it is part of the process of becoming yourself and not just going along with the path of your parents.

I went to a private Anglican high school in Nassau. We went to mass twice a week at school and took a required class in Religious Knowledge. That was when I was exposed to the teachings of Jesus, as we studied and broke down the meaning of parables and passages within the New Testament. I liked the story of Jesus and really resonated with him and his message. Yet, the desire to attend church did not emerge until I was much older and the mother of three sons. It was my yearning for a like-minded community to support me and my parenting these boys that inspired me to attend Unity Church of Charleston. I finally found a 'church' that resonated with my own beliefs about God and spirituality.

The practice of Yoga reemerged in my life when I moved to Charleston, SC, in 1986. There was one yoga teacher in the city at that time. His name was Thomas McMiniman, which he later changed to Michael Thunder. He was awesome. The class was only once a week, but it was an intimate and committed group of students and the experience led me to a deep appreciation for the practice of yoga and meditation. While my exposure in college felt more academic, this was truly the practice of yoga and I loved it. I was home.

I remember one particular experience in class that was undoubtedly one of those moments of Awakening that propelled me forward in my spiritual awareness. Thomas told us that we would be holding a posture for fifteen minutes. It was, for me, my most challenging posture, which was the forward bend. To do this posture, you sit on the floor with your legs together straight in front of you, you stretch your arms up and then bend forward at the waist, keeping your back straight, with the intention of bringing your abdomen towards your thighs. Eventually your whole torso touches your legs. This posture was intensely uncomfortable for me all along the whole back of my body. Thomas had been preparing us for this type of challenge through our weekly practice of breathing, meditation, and remolding our concept of pain into nonjudgmental awareness of the sensation in the body without labeling it as pain or resisting it. This was an epiphany for me that has become a powerful tool for dealing with many situations in my life that we would typically describe as painful, whether physical or emotional.

The awakening that I experienced lasted for only a minute or two. It was fleeting, yet deeply profound. Along with the rest of the class, I struggled with the posture and went through all kinds of inner resistance to this intense sensation that I previously called pain. He gave us pillows to put on top of our thighs that we could lean into as we slowly moved forward, breathing into the sensation and attempting to relax and move a bit deeper into the posture with each breath. All of us were groaning and breathing loudly and even crying at some point. Fifteen minutes is a very long time to hold a posture like this. Yet, we were supported by the environment, the words of our teacher and our collective commitment to this process.

By the last three to five minutes, all resistance in my body and mind had let go of me, and I was completely folded over in a full forward bend, my abdomen and chest resting relaxed on my outstretched legs. I went from feeling discomfort from bending slightly forward to complete surrender in the full bend, with no pain! It was a miracle. I moved into a state of ecstasy and a deep awareness of my Oneness with God, and All that Is. I felt at one with the molecules that made up all of life. I was aware of the vibrational frequency and nature of my own being and the way it was a part of everything that surrounded me and beyond. I was aware of my body being vibration and that it was no different from my spirit. As I felt this pure Awareness, there were no words for it, as I am offering now. It was a sense of absolute knowing. It was the first time I ever felt this Awake to my True Self, and while it only lasted for a few fleeting moments, it transformed me and set the tone for my spiritual unfolding from that moment on. I had peeked a glance at the magnificence of Life and my place within it, and there was no going back. The intense 'contraction' of the yogic asana propelled me into a blissful and profound expansion and Awakening. All resistance fell away at that moment, physically and mentally. In that complete surrender, the ability to perceive and experience the Divine reality flooded in. That awareness never went away, and yet the tangible experience of it would continue to elude me for many years to come.

6

Love, Art and Independence

MET MY HUSBAND, SHERMAN, ON a city bus in Columbus, Ohio. I was visiting my mother there in the summer of 1984 after I had finished my first year at the University of Windsor. I worked for the first month of summer vacation and decided to relax the second half before returning to the grind of academia. I was just seventeen years old. He was twenty-one. It was a sweet and passionate summer of love. He was beautiful, romantic, creative, interesting, and we had lots of fun together. We were undeniably drawn to each other. We spent almost every day together that summer. It was truly the blossoming of my womanhood and my self-expression as an artist was enlivened and aroused by this new sensuous and sexual awareness. My art was wild and bold and way outside the lines of the academic world of my art school.

After my summer of love, awakened to the passionate self

27

within me that had been dying to get out, along with my new approach to painting without rules, unabashed and bold, I lost my desire to be in the academic world and yearned to explore my art through the living of life. This was when I decided to leave University and join my sister Sarah in Boston.

Although I felt a magnetic and powerful connection to Sherman when he visited me in Canada once I returned to school, I began to feel scared and unready for the intense feelings we had for each other. I was so young and inexperienced and was threatened by his intensity and his confidence in what he wanted. He knew he wanted to be with me, and I was not so sure at that point. So I pulled away from him, and we went our own ways for the next year or so.

In my new home in Boston, I plunged into a life of painting and working jobs to support myself. My art expressed the unworldly dimension that I was so drawn to. I felt alive and guided when I painted. The more I got out of the way, the more God showed up in my art. At least it is how it felt to me. My work became more and more abstract. No longer concerned about the approval or opinions of others, my work exploded with color and sensuality. The paintings were vibrating with an intensity and life force that was beyond my own. I was prolific and painted almost daily during this time. I liked to work big, stretching my own canvases that were too big to fit in anyone's car. I didn't concern myself with such practical matters though. I was focused on creating and feeling the freedom of that.

Remembering back, however, I did not feel happy. I felt lonely in my solitary work and yearned to be connected to more people. It was not easy to make friends that were like-minded without the built-in social network of school life. I struggled terribly with the extremely long and cold winters.

I only made it through two winters before my life would take another interesting turn.

Sherman slowly came back into my life. He called. We reconnected. He visited me in Cambridge. He enlisted in the US Air Force. We started to see each other long distance, and we fell in love again. Maybe it wasn't all that slow, because within a year of rekindling the flame, we were married, and I was moving to Charleston, SC, where he was stationed to live and work.

We decided to get married for the convenience of it all. I was struggling to make ends meet as an artist working part-time for minimum wage, and a foreign friend of mine propositioned me to marry him for a fee, to enable him to get his green card. I was so young and naive that I was actually thinking about it. I hated to ask my parents for help, and we needed to fill the oil tank for much-needed heat for the winter. It seemed like a feasible way to make some extra money. I shared my thoughts with Sherman, and he nonchalantly offered that I marry him, and that he would send me the money he received from the Air Force for having a 'dependent.' Also, it would enable me to have healthcare, and we could fly around the world on military hops. Wow! That seemed like a better arrangement than marrying a guy that I would have to fake being in love with. At least I was in love with Sherman, although I was not ready to get married for real. As a matter of fact, I did not much believe in or have much respect for the institution of marriage at the time. My mom had been married three times by then, and I felt people were lured in by this unrealistic fantasy about marriage that just seemed too traditional and disempowering to women in particular. So, to marry for such a practical reason made more sense to me. Of course, we needed to keep it a secret so that other people would not try to make it into something it was not . . . a real marriage.

So we did it! On a very, very cold day on February 13th, 1986, we suppressed giggles as we irreverently said our vows. My sister was the witness, and the only other person I shared this arrangement with was my Mom. Mom and I had a very close relationship, and in many ways, we were more like friends than mother and daughter. Of course, I asked her not to tell anyone. We did not want to hurt anyone's feelings nor did we want to try to explain what we were doing. To us, it was not a real marriage.

I went to visit Sherman in Charleston, where he had been stationed, a month or so later, and I fell in love . . . with Charleston. I decided to move. I was miserable in the cold North and yearned to be warm again. I was in love with this man, and he was living in a beautiful tropical land. Seemed like a great idea. I did not make the move until the end of the summer, after I completed teaching at an art camp.

Unfortunately, my mother, in her excitement and who knows what else, leaked the news of our marriage to my grandmother and Sherman's mother, who lives in Columbus. It spread like wildfire, and we were thrown into an awkward quandary. Sherman's mother was understandably hurt and did not apprehend our motives, nor why he would keep it a secret from her. I was then confronted with needing to tell the rest of my family before they heard about it through the grapevine.

I remember visiting with my father and stepmother, whom I called Nana, in Windsor that summer to let them know that I was married to Sherman and would be moving to live with him in Charleston in a couple of months. At the same time, my sister Sarah let them know that she was a lesbian. It is quite comical actually when I think back to it all and how our parents must have felt. Now that I am a mother, I have a bit more insight as to how to handle the roller coaster rides our children take us on. I have learned that the best course of action is to do our best to enjoy the ride and try not to take things too seriously. I am still in the process of learning that now. Our parents took it very well and seemed to be very accepting of our life choices.

Charleston was indeed a hidden treasure at the time when I moved there in 1986. It was a coastal city with beautiful architecture, well persevered by the strict rules for historical preservation. It was a very affordable place to live. The beaches were lovely and easily accessible. Traffic was not at all congested. I was able to quickly connect to the arts community and feel a part of my new home. Shortly after I arrived, I helped organize an art show for the Moja Arts Festival, showcasing African-American and Caribbean art and culture . . . right up my alley. I felt like I had something to offer this community, as well as it did for me.

I started my first business in the open-air marketplace downtown. I made clay earrings that I painted, for my first product, along with displaying some of my paintings. It was a bit of trial and error to figure out what would be the best approach and product to sell in this environment. After several months, I decided to ask Dad and Nana for a $500 business loan, and I went out and bought a sewing machine at a pawnshop without even knowing how to sew. Sherman showed me how to thread the bobbin! I bought some fabric and cut patterns freehand to sew pants and simple skirts and dresses that I would then tie-dye to sell in the Market. This was the ticket to my success. I would prepare all week, from making the clothes and dying them, to then selling them on the weekends. Eventually, I found a seamstress to do the sewing, and I would do the tie-dying. When Sherman was home from traveling for the Air Force, he would help me tie-dye.

Within time, we added more products to our business. I began to go to New York to trade shows to find unique, ethnic lines of clothing and jewelry to sell, and Sherman would bring back Kenya bags and ebony carvings from his trips to Africa. It became such a lucrative endeavor, that once Sherman's first term of duty was complete, he left the Air Force and joined me in the Market business. I continued to paint and was involved in many art exhibitions. Life was good.

Sherman and I grew into each other and grew up with each other. It was not always easy, and often I felt myself wanting to flee the intensity and work of being in a relationship. I went through a lot of ups and downs and often felt like a feather in the wind. I was not creating my own reality, at least not consciously anyway. I was affected by the conditions of his behavior, my perception of his behavior, my mood, the time of the month, the moon. My happiness was in the hands of something outside myself that I could not begin to name. It was a fickle reality, and I knew that I wanted freedom from this pain-pleasure cycle more than anything.

I remember one day calling my mother crying and lamenting my anguish. I shared with her how lonely I felt, even as he sat right there with me. My mother lovingly and sternly coached me, reminding me that I had myself and that I created my own reality, and therefore, when I made the shift in perception within, then my outward reality would shift to reflect it. This was one of those Awakening moments. I sensed the profound truth in her words and felt a glimmer of the freedom I yearned for. It would be many years of practicing mindfulness, cultivating my awareness of my thoughts and the point of attraction that they held for me, along with dozens of inspirational books and spiritual teachers, for me to begin to truly *realize* the Awakening I sensed that day.

I realize that the blossoming and beautiful evolution of my relationship with this wonderful man is primarily because of the intense inner work that I have done. Of course, he has done his own work and has evolved as well in his own way, but the truth is, he became the reflection of my own point of attraction, my own inner work and the reality that I was creating. Relationships offer the most fertile ground for personal growth and spiritual awakening. The intensity of emotions that arise from the interactions that we have with those we love and care about most, offer us the opportunity to become aware of where we are relative to our connection to our Divine Self. Relationships with our lovers, parents, siblings and children inspire a vast range of emotions from blissful love, joy, ecstasy and gratitude to deep worry, fear, anger, jealousy, frustration, depression and despair. One of my beloved teachers, Abraham, describes this as our 'emotional guidance system'. Our emotions let us know if we are in alignment with our True Self, our Source, based on how good or lousy we feel. When we are feeling emotions of well-being, we are in alignment with Source Energy. When we are feeling bad, it indicates that we are thinking thoughts that are out of alignment with Source. I like the word Source or Source Energy to describe what we have traditionally given the name God. It feels more universal and expansive to me, without the limiting preconceived concepts of religious dogma.

This has been a very effective tool for me in my process of awakening. I have come to understand that my thoughts precede my emotions, but so often I am not aware of the thoughts, which seem at times to be thinking me. For me to become more mindful of my state of mind, I have sharpened my awareness of the signals my feelings are offering. My emotions are the first manifestation of a thought. Now when I am feeling off, I get still, breathe and check in with what is going on in my thinking that is making me feel this disconnection from my natural state of well-being. When we feel bad, we are always thinking a thought that is not in alignment with what our Source knows or feels about a condition. It takes vigilance to watch our thoughts and care enough about how we feel to catch a negative pattern of thought before it gets enough momentum to cause unwanted manifestations.

Again, the first manifestation of our thinking is our feelings. This is the point when we can most easily redirect the trajectory of a thought if it is not what we want to be feeling, and thus experiencing. Once the negative feelings are really strong, then the path back to alignment is a bit longer, but that is okay because no matter what, we can always find our way again, and we are continuously moving forward. The contractions may be more uncomfortable, and the labor may be longer, but the birth must happen, and we will be realigned with our Divine Self and the perspective that is one with Source.

I share this to give you an idea of the process that has evolved in me and very much has been inspired as a result of the relationships of love in my life. The early years with my husband were the perfect and blessed training ground that would prepare me for the most significant challenge of my lifetime—motherhood.

7

Becoming a Mother

B IG DEEP BREATH. WHERE DO I begin?

First of all, I had no idea what I was getting into when I was preparing for the birth of my first child. I was so meticulous about knowing everything I possibly could know about pregnancy and childbirth, maybe even somewhat obsessive. Others might describe me as being conscious. Yet from inside of my mind, I was full of worry and concern and perfectionism and information. I was also very excited and wanted to do what was best for my unborn child. I read about everything, and as a result, had many more decisions to make than the average woman who allows herself to be led through the process by her healthcare practitioner. I started out by choosing to go with a nurse-midwifery practice, which was lovely, but near the end of the pregnancy, I had learned about other options that felt more in keeping with my temperament.

I remember going to the hospital to see where I would be giving birth. First of all, the hospital was at least a thirty-five-minute drive from our house and required driving over two drawbridges. Second of all, it was a room in a hospital where I was to give birth. Neither of those conditions appealed to me. Having studied about the importance of the environment for a positive and safe outcome for the delivery, I felt it would be better for me to have a home birth with a midwife attending. I told Sherman as we walked away from the hospital that day that I just couldn't give birth in there, and he sighed and said, "'Don't do this to me, Beki.'" I smile when I write this, because of the resignation I remember hearing in his voice. He knew there was no arguing with me. He was a pretty traditional guy living with a woman who always seemed to question everything about the status quo. But, what I loved about him then and still do now, is his open mind and adaptability and flexibility, even if his initial response is resistant.

He adapted. I researched more and more and then plunged into the world of 'alternative' birthing, and thus parenting. It was a whole different world of alternative thinking and conscious people that became a part of my parenting process and defined many of the choices I made along the way that were outside the norms of popular culture and guidelines. It was not the easiest path to take, but the only possible one for me. I was guided, and my gut instincts were leading the way.

During my labor, I accessed the wisdom in the Awakening I experienced in my yoga class years before. I did not judge the sensations rippling and roaring through my body as pain but remembered to focus on it as energy and sensation. I went back, in my mind, to the day we held the forward bend posture for fifteen minutes. I practiced opening and relaxing into the birth in much the same way, being mindful of the contracting thoughts that would make the pain unbearable. I would quickly shift to make sounds that felt more expansive, which would release the tension and resistance to the intense flow of energy that was propelling my son forward. It was incredibly empowering to give birth in my own room, in a space that was prepared consciously for this sacred event. The environment was calming and beautiful, with paintings especially chosen to be in the space for this sacred emergence. Soft music played. My sister Joanna videotaped. My mother squirted oil on my perineum as the midwife instructed. Sherman supported and held me, keeping me from falling off the bed from my squirming with the unbelievable intensity of the energy flowing through me. It was uncomfortable and powerful and beautiful and utterly heart opening.

The birth was relatively quick for a first-timer with just two and a half hours of active labor. However, I had a head start. At seven months, when I decided to have the home birth, the nurse midwife I was with until then, examined me to check to see that all was well. That is when we discovered I was already in the early stages of labor—one centimeter dilated and fully effaced. I was instructed to get an ultrasound so they could check the measurements to make sure of the baby's development, which is when I found out that Chaz was a boy and not a girl, as I had been informed from an earlier ultrasound. Initially, I felt devastated since I had been relating to the baby as Zoe and was mentally prepared for the birth of my daughter. Not only did I have to adjust to the 'new' gender of my child, but I was also instructed to go on bed rest for six weeks to slow down any possible progression of labor. It was my first big challenge with motherhood and would be an indication of the true nature of parenting I would later experience. Parenting is unpredictable and has rendered me helpless and out of control over and over. It was a profound surrender that occurred within me during that period of bed rest. I felt great in my body but was required to stay horizontal, literally, for six weeks. All my attempts to control this pregnancy and birth and then this!

It was a huge lesson, and yet it would take many, many years of mothering to realize the power of surrendering and allowing the Divine Process to take over. Little did I know that this son would continue to be the teacher of this lesson. Over and over again, I would be reminded, by his very nature, that I cannot control the eternal flow of life—that life will have its way with me and so will the powerful beings of light that I gave birth to. I would be challenged to surrender over and over again in so many small and big ways. I would learn to trust in Divine Guidance, in him and in me. The alternative became unbearable. The resistance no longer being an option, gives way to the greatest and most delicious expansion, born of deep, and at times, desperate desire.

On May 15, 1993, my perfectly perfect son, Chazaray Marley Crowell Evans, was born, and my life took a 360-degree change. At this point, we had two businesses going, with Beki's in the Market and our two-year new business, Utopia, a contemporary boutique and gallery. Then, on top of that, during my pregnancy, Sherman got involved with a record company that he later took over, after Chaz was born. It was a juggle, but the biggest juggle of all was this new little human being with a personality and voice bigger than life. He consumed me, my life and all my energy.

The nursing was unexpectedly excruciating, and the sleep deprivation was beyond endurance. The intense demand of an infant and his need for my constant attention was utterly shocking! I had no idea. I was so conflicted by my feelings of love, adoration and awe, along with feelings of exhaustion, resentment and even depression, that I was consumed with guilt for not being happier. It made no sense to me. I was miserable and in love all at once. I was on the roller coaster of pleasure and pain, and it made my past relationship challenges with Sherman fade in the background. Of course, he experienced a great deal of my misery. I held him responsible for it at times. I realized, in retrospect, that I must have been suffering from postpartum depression. It was something I struggled with for the whole year after giving birth to both of my first two sons. Although I was prepared with my third son for the probability of it, I was blessed to experience what it is like not to be in such a crazy state of mind after having a baby, with him. The conditions were different ten years later and less stressful this third time, but I had also grown considerably in my spiritual process of awakening, which allowed me to perceive the experience very differently.

Chaz was a particularly demanding baby and child. Interestingly enough, a lovely woman named Carolyn Kfoury, who did a Reiki healing session on me while I was pregnant with Chaz, prophesied his temperament to me at that time. I remember her saying he would be a 'high demand child', having no idea what she really meant by that. When he was born, she led a God Mothers ceremony for him and gave him a gift of a big white feather with some crystals attached to it with a blue ribbon. Ironically and sadly she made her transition into nonphysical on Chaz's second birthday, just a few short months after a diagnosis of breast cancer. I truly believe that she is an angel now and sense that she may be a part of my son's spiritual guidance. The white feather is a symbol to me of her angelic wings.

Chaz was an intense being and desired a freedom that

the helpless body he had just entered into was incapable of giving him. It seemed to me that he was frustrated by his limitations, and as a result, he quickly began to master the faculties of his new body. Chaz walked at ten months, was dribbling a basketball by the age of one, rollerblading by two and riding a 'falling bike' (one without training wheels) by the time he was three years old! He wanted to be outside with the neighborhood kids all the time and begged, well before he could talk, to go out there with them. He would just grunt and point through the window with eagerness and frustration.

Regardless of his demanding nature and the sheer exhaustion that both of us felt, we were completely in love and enthralled by the magic of this beautiful being. Even in the fog of my sleep deprived postpartum haze, I recognized this son of mine as my 'Guru.' I sensed that his presence would be a powerful catalyst for my spiritual growth. Twenty-one years later I can tell you that this is the truth of my experience. When I think of the word guru, I think of a being who facilitates Awakening, a teacher and example of an Awakened being. The approach each guru takes with his/her disciples depends on what is needed. Of course, in this case, I do use the word metaphorically, recognizing that on some level we are all Awakened, and that part of him has offered the conditions of contrast to bring forth a great deal of awareness within me.

I believe that this son in particular came into this life knowing, prior to incarnation, that his role in my life and his father's would facilitate powerful expansion and awareness. Many of the experiences we have had with this son have been some of the most intense contractions of this lifetime. At times, my resistance has been tenacious, causing an insurmountable amount of pain and angst, prolonging the birth of new desires that have arisen from the contrasting experiences that only life can elicit. At other times, I have accessed my inner wisdom and guidance, using the many tools garnered along my path, and have felt the expansion and love and exhilaration that comes from breathing through a contraction and allowing for the movement forward to flow without effort or resistance. Those were the times when I was able to see the Truth of my son, regardless of the conditions that surrounded him. I could see his well-being, his divinity, his perfection in that very moment. Those were the times when I was not distracted by the illusions of his human experiences that were defining his desires and expansion to *his* path.

This is the child that made me a mother and the person that has stretched me most, introducing the most blessed contrast to affect the most intense focus and mindfulness within me for the purpose of expansion and freedom from the tyranny of my un-investigated thoughts. This is the child that has carried the heaviest burden in our family; for his inner guidance called him away from what was safe and comfortable and away from what his worried, but well-meaning parents wanted for him. He yearned for a different kind of adventure that pushed against what our society deems acceptable. All the while, his heart was pure, and love filled him as he dipped into dark corners of altered states with disconnected souls. He explored the treacherous fields of drug use and the risk of losing his mind to awaken to something beyond this dimension. He did lose his mind a few times, tinkering with insanity and somehow made it back to this world in one piece.

It is *his* path, a path that I have struggled to honor with consciousness and unconditional love since he was just a little boy. It has only been recently that I have found the path to my own freedom and understanding of true Unconditional Love. For too long I have been fixated on *his* path and perceived it from the flawed place of being disconnected from my own path and alignment with Source. For too long I was mesmerized by his drama, his choices and our reaction to them, his father's reactions and the difference between his and mine. It was torture.

Awakening is often inspired when deep surrender occurs after a 'rock bottom' experience when holding on to the illusion of control is simply no longer possible. This is the sensation of GRACE. It is such a sweet moment when you realize that letting go of control allows the Divine Guidance that has been lovingly, patiently waiting for this blessed moment to step in and take the reins. For me, this has happened many times in my life, and yet, there is one time in particular that was so dramatic and beautiful that my life has never been the same since.

But, before I share this powerful and expansive moment in my life, a little bit more on mothering.

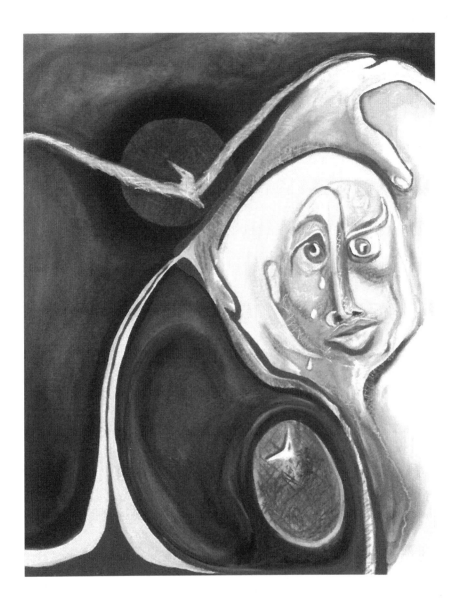

8

After the First Year of Motherhood

I REALIZED THAT AFTER THE FIRST year of becoming a mother that I needed to do something different or I was going to wither away into oblivion. For the first time since I had become an artist, I had gone a whole year without painting. Before becoming a mom, I painted weekly. It was an integral part of my life. In my desperate need to revive my spirit, I fled to my mother's downtown art studio, where she painted and taught art classes. She offered that I use it twice a week while she took care of my baby. It was the beginning of a dynamic and prolific expansion after a long, intense contraction.

Even though the first year of mothering was challenging, as I struggled with what many mothers deal with after the hormonal crash of pregnancy, along with the psychological issues of juggling the new responsibility, it was also a beautiful and heart opening experience. I was full of love and joy and admiration of this new being that had entered our life, and at the same time the struggle was complex and laced with guilt for feeling depressed and overwhelmed. The truth is that I felt completely blindsided and utterly shocked by the lack of freedom that having a child meant. I could not go anywhere or do anything without making arrangements for this dependent, helpless being. I could not even close my eyes unless he was asleep, which did not seem like much back then. The sleep deprivation was unbelievable! I just had no idea how much one little human being could demand of us.

I was so grateful to have the place of refuge and time to be by myself again when I entered the studio. I ordered several large 60"x 48" canvases and began to paint myself back into sanity. I created a large body of work over the next year that was a pure expression of the expansion and beauty that had been gestating within me during the time I was learning how to be a mother. I learned a valuable lesson during this time, realizing that to be a good mother, we have to take care of ourselves first, not unlike the instructions given on airplanes when we are told to put the oxygen mask on ourselves before assisting someone else. If we are not connected to our own Source of sustenance, then we have nothing really sustainable to offer another. This became a critical 'rule of thumb' for me when it came to parenting. For mothers, in particular, it has been our legacy to sacrifice in the name of our children, our families. For generations, mothers have put themselves last, and now I feel we are finally beginning to understand the detriment of this behavior. "One that is connected to Source has more power of influence than a million who are not." (Abraham)

Creating art is a way that I easily and directly connect to Source. It is a sacred process by which I intentionally get out of the way and allow the Divine Energy to flow through me. If I were able to stay consistent with my painting during that first year, would I have been able to avoid the angst and feeling of disconnection I felt during that time? Anyway, I am not sure if I could have painted, even if I had the time and space to do it. The intensity of focus that I had on this new son was all consuming, and the compression of my being was a powerful condition for my expansion. I can see clearly now that the process was exactly as it needed to be. I gained so much awareness during this time. The way in which a mother inherits a legacy of how to be a mother, unconsciously regurgitating the process, even though it may be archaic, caused a strong contraction within me, enabling a very powerful desire to be born. I wanted to be able to be a mother and still feel free! Seemed like an oxymoron, but it became my quest and my spiritual practice. I realized that it was the greatest gift I would give my son, and later all my sons: to be ALL of me, awake, joyous, free and connected to my Divine Self. It is the greatest gift any of us can offer anyone . . . our own alignment. This is truly Unconditional Love.

That time in the studio brought me back to life, back to my Self. The fog began to lift as the oxygen was restored to my being. My breath became deep and rejuvenating. Color filled the studio, with one painting after another revealing a new expression of my Divine path. Images of mothering, wombs, vulvas, the essence of woman and sensual sexuality blended within the organic images of flowers and nature. This body of work would make up a significant portion of a one-woman show of over forty paintings that I would exhibit in the Bahamas two years later.

I offer this story to inspire the awakening in mothers who may still feel mired in the obligatory, self-sacrificing approach to mothering, to allow themselves their freedom and to do what they must to honor themselves above all else.

It is my experience that when I do this, I also recognize the interconnection of all of life. As I heal, those around me heal. As I am in joy, I affect joy around me. As I am well and balanced and at peace, then, and only then, can I inspire the well-being and balance and harmony around me, in the individuals I share my life with and in the world that I am One with.

Mothering became the most powerful trajectory of Awakening I could have imagined. It has been the most beautiful and expansive adventure, leading me into the most majestic landscapes of love, compassion and joy. Mothering has been the catalyst for magical journeys with splendid views and treacherous terrain. It has been the emotional minefield that has given birth to an untouchable peace, which from its burning core, gave rise to the most exhilarating passion!

There is not one thing I would wish to be different in this journey. I am grateful for all of it.

I have given birth to the most amazing, lovely, brilliant beings and have been blessed by their presence, their offerings, their wisdom and the friction that they have offered for the polishing of my own pearl. The warrior nature of Chaz has provided a beautiful balance of friction and love. The compassionate and gentle nature of Noah easily balances the energy within our home. Tender, open-hearted Kai soothes my heart with his love and adoration. I have been beyond blessed . . . blessed with the perfect blend of energies to allow for my expansion and keep me feeling nurtured and loved at the same time.

To be able to perceive my life from the Eagle's eye view, taking in the broad perspective allows me to see the perfection of all the brilliant aspects of my life, seeing the whole picture, rather than becoming tangled up in the drama of the moment. Having had an awareness of this perception has helped me to embrace each moment, knowing the perfection of it, knowing that on some level I have chosen it, even if I cannot see in that moment the full picture of this grand design.

9

EAGLE AWAKENING and Unconditional LOVE

IT WAS A BEAUTIFUL SPRING day, and I was walking in my favorite place in the world, James Island County Park, just a couple miles from my house. The park has paved paths winding through lush woods, along marshland lining the Stono River and a small lake for fishing and kayaking. I would walk most mornings through my path, contemplating life and connecting with nature. It was and still is a form of meditation for me . . . these walks.

On this particular morning, Chaz and Sherman had had an argument the night before. The tension in my house was thick and unbearable. Sherman wanted Chaz out of the house. There were so many times that Sherman wanted him out that it does not matter what the issue was so much. The tension and fear had been building for some time, and the lack of control that both of us felt for the well-being of this child was truly making us all crazy. Chaz was sixteen years old and in eleventh grade at the time. Usually, every morning, Sherman would drive him in to the small private school on Johns Island, the neighboring island. That morning, I said I would drive him. I did not want them anywhere near each other.

I woke up early after a fitful sleep, filled with anxiety and sadness. Wisely, I got dressed and headed to my sweet place of refuge to hopefully shift this dense energy I was feeling. As I walked through the canopy of trees along the familiar path, I just let the tears roll down my face. I felt that the burden I was carrying was going to crush me. My heart was breaking, my body was listless, but I just kept on walking. As I neared the end of my trail, I headed to the dock that overlooked an expanse of marsh and the river. I looked up, and for the first time that I can remember, I pleaded out loud, "Please God, give me a sign." Nothing else, just those words. I did not ask for any specific sign. I think I just wanted to know that I was not alone. I felt desperate and exhausted from the holding on . . . holding on to control, to my son, to my sanity, to hope.

As I walked slowly onto the dock, a huge bird swooped over me and landed just about six yards ahead of me on a lamppost. I looked up and was astonished to realize that it was a Bald Eagle! Wow, what a sign! I stood enthralled and amazed, looking around to see if anyone else was there to witness this rare occurrence. Nobody. All alone, I soaked in the beauty and majesty of this remarkable bird: its huge fluffy feathered legs, its large bright yellow talons and beak and its white 'bald' head and signature white tail.

I had never seen a bald eagle in the wild before. I was completely enraptured by its regal beauty. After ten minutes or so, I decided to move in a bit closer, prepared for the possibility of it flying away. As I inched closer, it opened its massive and majestic wings and took off gliding across the sky, and within seconds it crossed over the Johns Island Bridge. I was so impressed by the power and speed of its flight. I was left with a tingling sensation all over my body and felt an exhilaration that would have seemed impossible just moments before. Something began unfolding in me at that moment that I would later describe as a full out Awakening, which I was able to experience and sustain for many days. In the past, this kind of sensation of Awakening had only been a divine glimmer, lasting a few blessed seconds or minutes. Even right now as I write about this, I am feeling the cascading of tingling energy all through my body.

I left the park and headed home, aware of this amazing opening within my heart and my mind. I told Chaz to get ready for school and that I would be driving him. Cloaked in misery and heavy energy, he came to the car with his hood over his head and slouched into the seat beside me. Incredibly, I was unaffected by his gloomy state. This spontaneous Awakening was obviously an experience that I was not controlling. It was happening to and through me, and a sense of deep connection and liberation was enveloping me.

As we drove, I noticed a phenomenon occurring within my mind that I can best describe as an unraveling of thoughts that had been causing me a great deal of pain and angst. Thoughts like: "I am being a codependent mother. I should not take care of him so that he can grow up. He will never grow up. My son is going to be a drug addict, end up in jail, or worse, dead." The thoughts arose quickly in my mind, and instantaneously the realization of the falseness within the thought followed, and then I experienced the awareness of the thought releasing *me* within seconds.

If you are aware of 'The Work,' a process of investigating your thoughts by answering a simple list of four questions, created by a woman and in my opinion, an enlightened being, Byron Katie, then you would have an idea of what was occurring within me. It was a spontaneous Awakening of the mind. I was not doing 'The Work,' 'The Work' was doing me. This was not an exercise that I was doing to experience freedom, as I had previously done when doing 'The Work.' It was freedom flooding through every cell of my being as the thoughts arose and unraveled and fell away, one at a time, at lightning speed.

It is interesting to write about it now, five years later, because in truth it was a wordless experience. It was clearly a powerful transformation that was occurring, and I was blissfully riding the wave of Love that was replacing all limiting thought and vibration within me. As the distractions of all those thoughts that I had given so much power began to disappear, I became more and more aware of the Love that I am, and that everyone and everything is Love. It was a visceral and experiential knowing that I have never felt before, other than in fleeting glimpses.

Words are utterly limiting to describe this most expansive experience I have ever had, and yet it is all I have to share this powerful and profound Awakening. So I will continue the best I can at this moment in time. Within this new state of perception, I turned to look at my emotionally shutdown son, and all I could see was perfect beauty. I did not connect to his inner turmoil. I could only see the eternal truth of his being . . . his perfection. I now know that I was not distracted by the condition of his behavior, but seeing through the eyes of Source, I was able to see beyond the story that caused the pain and know that he was already whole, perfect, healthy and free. It was possibly the first taste of Unconditional Love that I ever had.

Of course, I thought I loved my sons unconditionally, but the truth is, few of us ever have experienced love without condition. Ironically, with those we love most, we struggle most with Unconditional Love. We want certain conditions to be present in order to be in a state of love—conditions such as healthy, happy, safe, polite, self-sufficient, compassionate, kind, helpful, respectful, sober, appropriate . . . the list goes on and on. We always say we love them no matter what, and that may be true. But are we in alignment with Love when the conditions do not meet our desires or expectations? Most of the time we are derailed when our child is sick or disrespectful or when our spouse is cold, angry or distant. To love unconditionally is not about anyone else, it is about me staying connected to the Me that *is* Love, regardless of the conditions that exist around me. Recently I received this new perspective of this overly used concept of Unconditional Love from the teachings of Abraham, and it has caused a profound shift in me and in my spiritual practice.

Unconditional Love is what I was experiencing that day. I was experiencing life through the eyes of Source, and it was mind-blowing. I remember turning to Chaz and touching his cheek, and I believe I said, "You are so beautiful. I love you, son." I felt full of love and was sincerely enthralled by his beauty at that moment. I could feel a bit of a thaw within him, and he softened his rigid body just a bit. I spoke little on that fifteen-minute drive to his school, except to exclaim about the beauty of the sky as we drove over the Stono River Bridge to John's Island. Feeling my aligned energy, my son seemed to relax a bit more. When I dropped him off, he was concerned as to where he should go after school, since his father wanted him out of the house, and he usually picked him up. I told him that my mother would come get him since I would be at work, and we would figure things out later.

Amazingly, I was in a pure state of bliss at this point. I met with my dear friend Adaire and my mother for breakfast afterward and shared with them my epiphany. I then went home and picked up one of my favorite books by Byron Katie: *A Thousand Names for Joy*. I opened to a page in the middle of the book that poignantly spoke of my truth about this relationship with my son and how I truly wanted to experience my relationship with him. I was so excited and on fire that I decided to share the passage with my husband and let him know what I was feeling. The thing that happened next was another miracle.

When I read to him and shared with him my true feelings and passion about approaching our son differently, I did not care about his response. I didn't require anything from him. I did not need him to agree with me or change his approach to match mine. I was unflappable! I was expressing and sharing unconditionally. I let him know how much I loved him and respected his approach to fathering this son, and that I would parent the way that felt authentic and true to me. When you are in alignment with Source Energy, the way I was that day, it is too powerful and beautiful to dispute. There is too much love present even to consider it. I felt his receptivity in a way I don't remember ever feeling it. That could have been because my perception allowed me to feel the best of Sherman, just as I perceived him to experience me in that way as well. I was not projecting my expectations of resistance within him. I was seeing him through the eyes of Source. A sweet intimacy was the result. Love was exploding from within me as we made love passionately. My heart was so open, and there was absolutely no fear or resistance within me and the vibration I was emanating. The freedom I felt was exhilarating.

I went to work in my lovely little boutique, Utopia, that day and joyfully interacted and connected with customers. This beautiful Awakening continued to expand within me. By the evening, my mother called to say she was going to pick me up from work, instead of Sherman. On the ride home, she broke the news to me of what had happened that day. My son had been accused of taking money from another student at school to buy him some marijuana. Mom said that Sherman was concerned that the news might throw me into a whirlwind. He worried that this intensely openhearted state he witnessed in me that morning would make me more vulnerable than usual. While I can appreciate his concern, he was dead wrong. I was invincible within this aligned state of mind and being that I was experiencing.

Now, normally I would have been a basket case. My fear would be triggered, and I would feel sick in the gut and completely anxiety-ridden. The oh so familiar worry would take over my mind and I would live this way for who knows how long. Instead, I was filled with love and compassion. Miraculously, the joy I felt was untouched by this 'condition.' When I walked into the house and back to Chaz's room, there was an ominous aura permeating the house. He was lying face down on his bed. I sat next to him and caressed his back as he wept into his pillow. I smiled and told him that I loved him, that he was deeply loved, that he was safe, that he *was* love, perfect and whole. I stroked his sweet soft face, and all I felt was love, compassion and deep untouchable joy. Sherman came into the room and sat there watching us. I went to kiss him and asked him how he was doing. I remember little of the conversation, of the words that followed in the sullen space of that room. All I can now recall is this liberated sense of peace, this rare sensation of Unconditional Love. Nothing could derail me. If this catastrophic event did not occur at this time, I would not have known the profound significance of this Awakening. I am so grateful to have been confronted with a challenging condition within the midst of my awakened state, so that I could know the sensation so fully and completely that no matter how long it lasted, it would have an indelible mark on my being, never to be forgotten, transformed forever as a result of it.

The week continued with the conversation of our son and his future and how to handle it and how to control the conditions of his precarious life. His passionately committed father strategized to bring him to his lawyer friend to have a talk with him about the consequences of his actions and to caution him about potential future choices. I went along with the motions, not resisting anything, maintaining this inner peace and unflappable joy. I loved my son and loved my husband. I saw them in their perfection wholly, knowing the well-being of all of us. I understood Sherman's worry, fear and need to control. I knew it well and would know it again. But for that moment I was free . . . utterly and completely free.

It lasted for about a week, one glorious, unforgettable, profound week. In the past, I had experienced only a glimpse of the fleeting, yet undeniable, Awakened state. Now I have feasted on the bliss of Enlightenment, and I will never be the same. I will always be able to reach back to this palpable, visceral memory, and inform my present moment with this remembered awareness. I now know what is possible and I know that it is attainable for us all.

The last several years have been laced with pain, expansion, awareness, anxiety, worry, growth and epiphanies.

The saga of Chaz and his path has been the most intense and powerful catalyst for my spiritual journey of Awakening. Have I said already that he is my guru? He is the one that has offered me the most profound opportunities for the awareness of my limited beliefs, my hypocrisy and patterns of thought that have held me captive and kept me from a deeper truth and the realization of my wildest desires. As long as I required conditions that felt safe and comfortable in order to feel joyful, loved and peaceful, then I was living a shadow of the potential of the life I was meant to live. I was living a conditional life, which is not very creative and feels as precarious as the life my son was living . . . or at least my perception of it.

I remember being told once or twice when Chaz was a baby that you are only ever as happy as your saddest child. The statement appalled me. Little did I know that I would come to understand the truth of it, and yet I still refuse to believe it. I will not be a feather in the wind, experiencing life based on the unpredictable nature of situations and people beyond my control. To me, that is the hell that many of us are experiencing.

I am now committed to cultivating a state of being that reflects the Awakened state that my Eagle Sign from the Divine inspired in me. I choose to live my life Unconditionally—joy beyond condition, love without condition, untouchable peace, inspired passion. I am finding that when I am in this state of Alignment, the outside conditions reflect my inner condition. I want to live my life from the inside out. I do not want to *face* reality. I am choosing to *create* my reality.

It takes vigilance. I must watch my thoughts and pay attention to my feelings at all times. When I feel bad, I know that I am veering off of my alignment with the Source within me. If I care enough about how I feel, then I will not continue down the train of thought that is manifesting the undesired

59

feeling. My mantra is simply, 'Unconditional Love.' When I become aware of the feeling and understandable human tendency to react to an unwanted condition with resistance, allowing it to take me away from the sensation of Love, then I start my mantra, understanding the depth of its meaning to me. I have even become aware of resistance to feelings that I think I shouldn't feel, and I practice allowing the condition of my own unwanted feelings. I know. That is pretty heavy. You might have to reread that sentence. I realize that my own thoughts and feelings are at times as much out of my control as the behavior of another person. This is the perfect time to practice Unconditional Love, and sometimes I am able to experience equanimity, recognizing that all feelings are equal. No judgment. It's a hard one, yet when experienced, it is incredibly liberating.

What I know for sure is that all of this is a process. It is unending because we are unending, eternal beings born of the One Source and forever evolving. The wonderful author Khalil Gibran speaks perfectly of the nature of our purpose in *The Prophet*: "Our children are not our children. They are the sons and the daughters of Life longing for Itself." I read this book when I was a teenager and again and again throughout my life. I genuinely understood this passage more after reading *Conversations with God* by Neale Donald Walsh. His book explains that our purpose is to come forth into the physical, not to learn, but to experience. We are the part of God that is able to *experience* Itself. Without us and all of life, God simply Is. By creating us as seemingly separate from Itself, God is able to experience Life, Love, Itself, through us.

There are many books by this author, and I've loved them all and resonated deeply with the message. Reading them felt like coming home to something I had always known but had recently forgotten. There have been many incredible teachers that have influenced my spiritual path and awareness throughout my life and have offered life-expanding skills to navigate the mind-field of the human experience. I am sure that without them I would not have been so ripe for the Eagle Awakening or able to really integrate that experience into my evolving process of Awakening now. I am deeply grateful for them all and would like to offer you a glimpse into their message, just in case your heart sings with the recognition of the truth that lies within it. Inspiration is a beautiful and life-aligning thing to share.

10

Inspiration and Guidance

I HAVE LIVED ON THIS EARTH as Beki Crowell for forty-eight years . . . just enough time to look back at the whole of it and begin to gain a broad view, the view of an eagle in flight. Sometimes we become mired in the perspective that is right in front of us and lose the vision of the grand, divine, brilliant design. I imagine that we had a part in this design before entering physical bodies. I believe we have chosen the environment, people, region, and conditions of our life, because from this broad and divine perspective we are fearless and adventurous and know that there are no true risks, because there is no true death. From the realm of Spirit, we know our worthiness, and we are fully aware of our Oneness with the Source of all that Is. We do not play it safe when we chose our life-on-earth experiences, because we desire expansion.

Experience offers this expansion. 'Contractions' offer the momentum in the birthing process to catipult us towards our deepest and wildest desires.

When we come into this physical dimension where we forget our infinite and unlimited nature and the intentions we had proior to becoming human, we sometimes want to play it safe. We want to avoid the contractions, and when we realize that we can't, that life will expand no matter how much we resist, we ask for drugs. Anesthetize me, please! I feel that what we actually want to numb out is the pain that is a result of the resistance to what is. The resistance is so much more the problem than the actual reality. Resistance stems from our thinking. It is the screaming voice inside your head that says, "No way! This is not happening. This is not okay. This will kill me!" And yet, somehow women have given birth billions of times, for eons, without dying, with and without painkillers.

Even though humanity struggles through many atrocious conditions while living life on Earth, somehow we are still here, and even when are not, we will be somewhere else, because life is eternal, and when our bodies die, not only do we continue to live in Spirit form, but we are also liberated from the amnesia of our True Divine Nature—the amnesia that we willingly chose for the grander design of propelling life forward.

I already mentioned one of my teachers that has had a profound impact on me. She is probably more of a role model than a teacher. Byron Katie *shows* me what it looks like to live the way I lived that one week after the Eagle flew into my life. She experienced a spontaneous awakening at age forty-three, after ten years of deep depression. During that time she was suicidal, full of rage and afraid to leave her home. Finally, Katie checked herself into a halfway house, the only facility that accepted her, and she was placed in an attic room all alone, since the other residents were afraid to be around her. One day as she lay on the floor, not feeling worthy enough to even sleep in the bed, a roach crawled over her foot, and at that moment, she experienced a transformative shift in her consciousness, which she describes as 'waking up to reality'.

She describes her unexplainable experience in *A Thousand Names for Joy*:

> *I discovered that when I believed my thoughts, I suffered, but when I didn't believe them, I didn't suffer, and that this is true for every human being. Freedom is as simple as that. I found that suffering was optional. I found joy within me that has never disappeared, not for a single moment. That joy is in everyone, always.*

I experienced her in person at the Unity Church in Charleston. She came for the special event to share this process she calls 'The Work.' It was the first time I had heard of her. There were no books about her or by her at that time. She sat at the altar at the front of the church, on a chair with an empty chair across from her. We were given a worksheet with questions to answer, which we were encouraged to fill out. We were invited to come sit with her, so that she could demonstrate the process and so those witnessing could easily apply the process of inquiry to the issue that they wrote about on their paper.

As this process of inquiry unfolded, I was blown away. It was so simple and so profound. I remember one woman sitting with Katie, sharing her written statement about feeling as though she should be further along in her life at her age—

that she should be married, have children, have a better job, etc. Katie picked up a rose from the big vase of flowers between them. She looked at the beautiful red rosebud, not fully open, and said, "Open! Open! Why aren't you more like your friends?" She peered over at the vase of flowers, some of which were more fully in bloom. I swear, I wanted to weep. I looked at whomever I was with and said, "I can leave now. I got all I need." It was the profound truth of her simple statement; it was her awakened beingness, her absolutely loving presence that woke something up in me.

I will not go into the process of 'The Work' here. If your interest is piqued, I would highly recommend that you go to her website, www.thework.com, and explore more about her and the process of inquiry that has brought freedom and enormous relief to so many. She is invited to speak to large groups of people all over the world and to do 'The Work' with people in the audience. I love her books, especially *A Thousand Names for Joy: Living in Harmony with the Way Things Are*. I have kept it next to my bed for many years, and when I am going through a tough time, it truly is a Godsend, helping me to shift my perception and move beyond the painful thoughts that I identify with unconsciously.

It is said that after doing this process for a while, you are no longer doing 'The Work,' but 'The Work' is doing you. That was my experience, particularly after the Eagle Awakening I described earlier. The painful thoughts were literally unraveling within me, and the freedom was beyond anything I have ever felt before.

Another amazing teacher that is akin to the Katie phenomenon is Eckhart Tolle, author of *The Power of Now*, along with several other books. When I was exposed to this incredible book, I was coming out of a year of postpartum depression, after the birth of my second child, Noah. Realizing how my unmanageable state of being was affecting me, I came up with a new schedule with my husband that would allow me some relief and more freedom from the intense responsibly of our two young sons and the businesses. At that time, we had two retail stores and were developing a wholesale apparel company. Sherman was traveling a lot for his new business, and I needed to keep up with more than I could handle and at the same time maintain an inner balance. I later realized that I was experiencing the hormonal roller coaster ride of postpartum and that my perception of reality was affecting my emotional swings, or maybe it was the other way around. Nevertheless, I was grappling with my resentment over the way in which a mother tends to become the primary caretaker, regardless of the amount of other work each parent does.

In our case, the business we had at that time for eight years was the one that provided all our income. The new business, NuSouth Apparel, was an exciting and promising venture that was recieving international attention, and yet it was not creating any income at that point and required a great deal of attention, time and resources. At that time I was mostly responsible for our established boutique, Utopia, and he focused most of his energy on NuSouth.

I noticed that if I wanted to go out, I felt I needed to ask him to watch our sons, whereas when he was going out, he would just let me know, assuming my availability to take care of them. We slipped into this routine, partly because I began the relationship with the babies as the nursing mother, and they needed me for their sustenance. By the time they were eating food, the pattern was already set. I also feel that the societal legacy has always put mothers as the caretakers of the family and home, and so this traditional role is easy to slip into.

However, this is changing, and the relationship that fathers are having with their children is becoming more intimate as a result of their increasing involvement in parenting.

My moment of desperation for relief from the exhaustion of feeling so much anger and resentment, exasperated by the hormonal hell, prompted me to quietly and intensely propose an ultimatum to my beautiful husband, who simply had no idea of the magnitude of my misery. After showing him a list of the many responsibilities of running a household and my part in the businesses, I asked him what he did on the list.

The imbalance seemed obvious to me. I let him know that his presence at home, without his equal participation, made me feel angry and resentful, and I could cope better without him there. I proposed that he either move out or we make a major change. I must say here, that I was truly prepared for him to move out, even though I did not want to separate. I knew I loved him and wanted to be with him, but in my state of disconnection from my Divine Source, I was desperate. Something needed to change. I could not continue feeling this way any longer. This was another profound 'contraction' that would culminate into giving birth to the miracle we both desired.

Sherman agreed to a new schedule that consisted of us each being responsible for three days of being with the kids and preparing meals for them. The seventh day would be a family day. If there was a day or days that he needed to be out of town or wanted to go out, he would be responsible for making arrangements for them, whether it was asking me or getting a babysitter. Previously, he had never asked me to take care of the kids, because he just automatically assumed it was what I would do; whereas, I always asked him if I had something I would want to do. It was a double standard that every single one of my fellow mothers endured. This new arrangement helped to dismantle this pattern and recreate a new way of co-parenting.

In the beginning, it felt awkward, and I was rigid about the schedule. I would leave the house on my three days, even if I didn't feel like it. I had an art studio where I would go and often just sleep. Sometimes I would go to my mother's and sleep and rest and talk. I forced myself to leave Sherman with the boys alone, even when I wanted to stay, because I would end up taking over and doing the very things I wanted Sherman to do.

Out of my yearning for joy and freedom and regaining my inner connection to my True Self, something else as wonderful emerged. Sherman was becoming the most amazing father I know. He developed the most beautiful relationship with those boys. His commitment to them has been unfailing, and his involvement in their lives has been his priority. I feel, in a way, that in standing up that day and requiring this shift in our trajectory, was not only a gift to myself, but it was also a gift to Sherman and my sons. It became a powerful opportunity for a deepening of intimacy and connection in the relationship between two young sons and their father. The relationship that he now has with our sons is a big part of what makes our partnership so strong and loving. I feel so much gratitude to be with a man that loves us so completely. I have truly felt Unconditional Love with him and from him.

During this time, I started going to my art studio three evenings a week and sometimes during the day, if I could. This time spent in my studio became my healing ground. I slept and read mostly, not yet ready or aligned enough to paint. The books I read during this introspective time were healing for me and became a part of my spiritual evolution. The first one was *Conversations with God*, by Neale Donald Walsh. When I read this inspired book, a literal conversation between Neale and God, I was elated. I felt like the messages that were being channeled through Neale were indeed the words of Source, speaking a language that was clear and easy to assimilate. I completely resonated with the material, as though deep inside it was what I have always known to be true but could not have begun to find words to convey. It was soothing and reassuring and stimulating. I could feel myself healing the wounds of disconnection. I could breathe again and take in the depths of Truth that fed and nourished my soul. Slowly, the numbness began to give way to the tingling sensations of resonance that awakened me to Life again. I read *The Power of Now* next and felt the truth and profundity of Tolle's message.

Eckhart Tolle had a very similar experience to Byron Katie's. He was in an extreme state of mental and emotional anguish. He was suicidal and utterly lost when he experienced a spontaneous awakening, which he calls an inner transformation. He then spent many years as a vagrant before becoming a spiritual teacher, living "in a state of deep bliss," he says. His book, *The Power of Now*, opened my mind and cultivated a practice in me of becoming more mindful of the present moment. He offers a compelling case for the 'power of now' as the only true moment that anything is ever really experienced. There is only Now. Past and future are mental constructs: a perceived memory of reality or a perceived projection of a reality to come. He explains that, if we can become fully present in this eternal moment of now, all suffering and fear will be diminished and eventually erased. He speaks of enlightenment and awakening as a state that is attainable by all and offers a pointer to this truth.

One of my favorite teachings would be his description of

"clock time" and "psychological time." Clock time is when we are aware of the practical things that must be done within the construct we call time, such as picking up the children at school at 3 p.m. or being at work by 9 a.m., etc. It also includes learning from the past and predicting the future based on practical information. However, many of us tend to live and operate within psychological time, which Tolle describes as "identification with the past and continuous compulsive projection into the future." Psychological time can show up as repetitive thoughts that cause stress, anxiety and fear. It is when I am creating a whole stressful or even mundane story in my head about a thought that is keeping me from really being present in the moment.

An example of psychological time versus clock time would be on a day that I needed to pick up my sons at preschool, and I was running late. If I am not 'in the moment' and simply being aware of the practical aspects of clock time, then I may be consumed with the way-too-familiar mental chatter of psychological time: "What would they think of me, always running late? I feel like such a bad mother. Why can't I get out on time? Well, I will tell them at the school that the traffic was terrible and held me up. Maybe they won't charge me the late fee?" That kind of stressful, nagging chatter could go on for the fifteen minutes of the drive to pick them up, robbing myself of the peace of being simply present with what is. If I am in clock time, I will recognize that I may be a couple of minutes late and that is it. No story. I would apologize for being late. If I need to pay a fee for my tardiness, I pay. Simple. This then frees up an incredible amount of energy and mental space for creative thought to emerge.

That was such a revelation to me. I became aware of the way I lived in my mind more than I did in my life. The thoughts that kept me from being fully present were mostly mundane, repetitive and self-sabotaging. I began to watch my thoughts and realize the nature of my thinking and the way it made me feel. I read and read and read, soaking up all this profound wisdom and transforming my state of being. That year, after Noah's first year of life, was devoted to healing through reading, sleeping, meditating and I think I may have done some yoga during this time as well. The reading stands out the most, because prior to this time, I did not spend much time reading these types of books.

It felt as though I had been primed my whole life for this knowledge and that, up until that moment, I just was not ripe enough to take it in so fully so that I could bear the fruits of that ripeness, which I devoured with gratitude and deep relief. It was delicious! The profound contraction of another year of postpartum hell gave birth to a whole new state of awakening in me, allowing me to receive and process a great deal of esoteric, metaphysical and spiritual material that has very much informed my continuing and evolving spiritual journey of Awakening to the full awareness of my True Self.

I am not quite sure when exactly the book *Ask and It is Given,* by Abraham-Hicks, came into my life, but it became a long and lasting relationship that is still strong and thriving. The book was awesome, but what followed has been mind-blowing. Abraham is described as, "a group of consciousness from the non-physical dimension." They speak through the physical human being Esther Hicks and were inspired to come forth as a result of Esther's husband, Jerry's, asking and Esther's allowing. They say, "You are the leading edge of that which we are. We are that which is at the heart of all religions."

Simply said, they are pure positive energy coming forth

from a nonphysical dimension to offer us the most brilliant, beautiful, loving, empowering message to help guide all and any who resonate with the offering. I am one of the thousands, possibly millions who have benefited from this amazing offering. I have read many of their books and listened to dozens of their CDs of workshops that they offer all over the country throughout the year. I went to a workshop back in 2006 with my mother and a friend. It was an exhilarating experience. I still listen to the CDs in my car almost daily and a never-ending flow of wisdom, and practical application of that wisdom, is given to me as I absorb the love they share. All my sisters, my mother and many of my friends listen to the material and feel as inspired by them as I do. Others in my group of Abraham enthusiasts would agree with me when I say that reading and listening to the material is incredibly helpful in reprograming our thinking from the old limiting beliefs that have kept us separate from our Divine Selves to new beliefs that remind us of our connection to each other and to Source. This allows us to tap into our full potential, our true source of power, and to create the life of our deepest desires.

The practice of mindfulness that was inspired by Katie and Tolle was amplified and cultivated at another level when I delved into the teachings of Abraham. Abraham teaches that our feelings are our emotional guidance system that allows us to know where we are in relationship to Source Energy or our own Divine Self. When we care enough about our feelings to pay attention to them and recognize that they are offering us valuable insight as to our vibrational point of attraction, then we can begin to know what unconscious thoughts are creating the feelings. The feelings are the first manifestation of our thoughts. For so long, we have been encouraged to stuff our feelings or control them, and yet their purpose is to offer guidance and a signal indicating the trajectory of the thought and the pending manifestations. Simply put, when we are feeling good—joy, peace, clarity, love, enthusiasm, vitality, gratitude, etc.—then we are at the same vibrational frequency as Source. The further we are from the pure positive feelings, then the further we are from thinking thoughts that are in alignment with Source.

Now, just because we may be feeling negative emotions—sad, depressed, jealous, frustrated, angry, anxious—it does not mean that the energy that is Source has abandoned us. It means that we are thinking thoughts that hold us from experiencing the Oneness or alignment with Source. In a way, you can think of the feelings as a navigation system to let us know when we are straying from the higher vibrational frequencies of Source.

So why is it so important that I am in alignment with Divine Source? Well for one, it feels really good. And two, when we are in alignment with Source, we are allowing all the things we have deemed good to come into our experience—to be real-ized by us.

How does the Universe know what it is that we desire? The Universe doesn't know what we want because we have written it down, because we prayed for it or recited some affirmations—it knows well before we offer these actions. It knows because we have sent out "rockets of desires as a result of living in the contrast." When you know what you don't want, you become clear about what you do want, and you ask before you even realize you are asking. When you ask, it is given. Hence the title of their book, *Ask and it is Given.* Abraham adds to the sentiment, "one hundred percent of the time." So why don't we seem to be getting what we ask for? Well, because we are not aligning with the vibrational frequency of our desire. So the key is to get into a place of allowing. It is a three-step process:

> **Ask.** This happens automatically by living in the contrast, which defines desire.

> **It is Given.** On a vibrational level, your desires are being fulfilled, and the whole universe expands as a result.

> **ALLOW.** Do this by thinking thoughts that feel good. However, do not resist or supress any feelings as they arise. Allow and feel them and then gently refocus on a thought that feels better. Soothe yourself into alignment. Go downstream. Stop expending so much effort. As you release resistance you embody a vibration that matches your desires, and then your path will be realized by you in the physical realm.

I know, too simple to be real. Well, it is not always so simple to think thoughts that feel good. We have been trained into thinking so many thoughts and letting them run rampant in our minds, assuming we don't have much of a choice about what we think. We may not be able to control every thought we think, but we can become more mindful and give less and less airtime to the thoughts that make us feel bad. We don't have to believe everything we think either.

This goes back to the concept of Unconditional Love, which I spoke of earlier. I care so much about how I feel that I will not allow any condition keep me from my connection to Source. When we are in this elevated state of Unconditional Love—Byron Katie would say, "loving what is"—then we are in the ultimate state of *allowing*, which is the third and most important step of creating. The question is, will we create consciously or unconsciously? The fact is we are creating all the time, either consciously or by default. I am thrilled that I am the creator of my reality. Knowing this means that I never need to be a victim of my reality, that I am a participant in the creation of my experience. I know this can seem daunting at times. It is very important that we are careful not to beat up on ourselves when we are creating a reality that is seemingly not what we want. Why would anyone create a reality that is tragic and painful? I see it like this: we are either creating by default, without the awareness that our thoughts and actions have an impact on the conditions around us, or we actually want what we are creating. Usually, it is a mix of both. I believe that some of the most painful experiences in our lives are allowed to happen by our Divine Self, and maybe even orchestrated, as a way to bring expansion in our lives and in the lives of others.

I love Katie's philosophy: Loving What Is. She knows (for her, it is not belief) that whatever shows up is what she really wanted or it would not be here. Her vibrational stance is one of complete allowing, no resistance. I remember hearing her say something like this: "I love the smog in LA. I just breathe it in, knowing that each breath will bring me to the right and perfect time of my death." She does not speak so much of deliberate creating as Abraham does, and yet she is a living example of the type of surrender necessary to 'allow' the unfolding of the life we have created and desire to realize in our experience— the life we asked for and have been given. Now all we need to do is ALLOW and trust and watch the unfolding of our true desires, which are more perfect and expansive than we could have even imagined in our wildest dreams.

I feel like my current attention to practicing Unconditional

Love is the essence of all the spiritual teachings I have encountered. Earlier on, I shared that Abraham has helped to define Unconditional Love in a new way, and for me, it has been a transformational understanding. This bears reiterating in another way. It is the practice of allowing all conditions to be just as they are, not trying to control, manipulate or fix, which offers the greatest freedom. When I am allowing what is, I am loving what is . . . Unconditional Love . . . Unconditional living. No resistance. This is when I am able to experience the manifestation of my desires. This is how we create. The molding of the clay of our lives comes from living and experiencing and choosing and making a new decision about what it is we want or don't want. To fully experience the physical manifestations of our creations, Abraham teaches the Art of Allowing.

Over the years, they have offered many different ways to practice this art, all of which lead to the primary objective, which is to align yourself with Source. Abraham is fun, funny, full of joy, wisdom, love, enthusiasm, passion and clarity. I can't begin to express my gratitude to the forces of the Universe that have brought Abraham into my awareness.

The basic foundation of the Abraham teachings is grounded in the Universal Law of Attraction, which essentially is: "the essence of that which is like unto itself, is drawn." Like attracts like. What you think about is what you get. Your vibrational offering or stance equals your point of attraction. The Universe hears what you mean not what you say. It responds to your vibration, which is interpreted through your feelings. Again, your emotional guidance system indicates your vibrational stance. How do we change our vibrational point of attraction? By listening to our feelings and then shifting our attention to things that make us feel better; by not indulging in negative thinking, understanding that it has an impact on our current experiences as well as the ones around the corner. I will not indulge in complaining, judging, disappointing, worrying or anxiety-producing thoughts. When I become aware that I am going down that rabbit hole, I do my best to pivot my thinking before it gets too much momentum. Once the momentum of negative thinking has begun, I try to ride it out and not be too hard on myself for 'letting' it happen. You've got to love knowing that a good night's sleep helps to slow down the momentum and offers a new day to start over again.

The practice of Gratitude is a powerful tool for aligning your vibration with Source. I have practiced this for years in the form of a 'daily' email with a group of like-minded people. Cultivating the perspective of gratitude consistently, re-trains your thinking to see life through the eyes of Source. If you think about it, no matter what, you can find something to be grateful for: the air we breathe, nature, a roof over our heads, legs that carry us from here to there.

I remember when my sister Mary Beth, who is a part of my gratitude circle, was going through a really tough time. In the beginning, she rarely wrote, and when she did, it might be a few words. After some time, I noticed her starting to write more and more, eventually flowing with words of gratitude. Her emails became long and effusive and beautifully alive. She had been struggling with a new diagnosis of bipolar disorder, and I was wondering if maybe her medication had been changed to warrant the obvious change in her state of being.

Finally, after a few months, I called her and asked her what had changed. She said that her medication was the same. The transformation she was experiencing was a result of her reading dozens of transcripts from Abraham workshops that she had ordered. She had immersed herself in the material, which helped her to climb out of the dark hole of her depression. She now regularly listens to the CDs and has shared many with me as well. The Abraham effect is truly amazing.

These teachers have profoundly enriched my life, and what I have shared with you here, only skims the surface of what they have to offer. There are many ways that lead us to the life we desire. The paths are countless, and at the end, we will all be in the same place, reunited with our Divine Self and with the Source of All That Is. We are all destined to know our magnificence, our Oneness with God. I feel that each of us must follow the path that resonates with us most and makes our heart sing. If we do, then the road will be less arduous, and yet an arduous journey is okay too. It is just good to know that we have a choice. It doesn't have to be so hard. Life is meant to be fun and joyful, an adventure of freedom and love expressed and felt.

As Abraham says, "The basis of life is freedom, and the purpose of life is joy."

11

12 STEPS and Ecstasy

I N 2013, I HAD A powerful shift in my spiritual process of Awakening when I decided to participate in a twelve-week *12 Steps to Awakening* group. A friend of mine, whom I very much respect, was facilitating it at my church, Unity of Charleston. His name is Duke Warren, and he played an essential role in my son Chaz's life when he was exploring the world of drugs and mind-blowing awareness. Duke was his counselor from the tenth to twelfth grade. He had been in recovery (Alcoholics Anonymous) himself for forty or more years, and he is a spiritual seeker with certifications in several different therapy modalities, including 'The Work' by Byron Katie. He is also very much a proponent of meditation.

When Chaz was in the psychiatric hospital for ten days after taking the drug Ecstasy, Duke came to see him almost every day. Sherman and I were there for all the visiting hours, twice a day, and when Duke would get there, Chaz would say, "Come on Duke, let's go meditate." They would go in his room, and Duke would lead him into a guided meditation. What I particularly appreciated about Duke was that he was always able to see the divine aspect of Chaz, even in the middle of the human muck we were all wading through. He would say to me that he believed Chaz had the potential to be awakened in this lifetime.

While he was in the midst of this harrowing psychotic bout, Sherman and I were drowning in our fear and disbelief, contemplating the worst, not knowing if we would have a permanently brain-damaged son or some other variation of a horror story. Seeing my son in his innate well-being felt impossible at that time, although I knew it was necessary. I had been worrying about him his whole life. Now the emotional strain was practically unbearable. I woke up with panic attacks daily. I cried in my sleep and my gut was in knots. I felt so confused and completely out of my element. Yet again, this time of intense contraction was another powerful point of propulsion forward in my spiritual life.

Along with Duke, who was in Recovery, Divine Grace would offer me the loving guidance of my dear friend Adaire, who had been in recovery for about twenty-five years. They were both very much a part of the recovery community in Charleston and had an in-depth understanding of the transformative power of the 12 Steps, originally designed for Alcoholic Anonymous, but used by many different groups to help heal addictions. Adaire has a son the same age as Chaz, and they were friends when this event occurred. Both Adaire and her son were in the middle of our drama, and it was Adaire that Chaz confided in about taking the ecstasy. She is the one who brought him to the emergency room a whole week afterward. She stayed with us throughout the entire process, offering her love, wisdom, understanding and comfort. She and Duke continued to support Chaz after he came home and made an effort to stay clean and go to AA and NA (Narcotics Anonymous)meetings daily. He was only seventeen years old at the time, and the 'rooms' of AA had few young people in them, which made it challenging for him to continue on that path for very long. But he tried, successfully attending 90 meetings in 90 days. Yet, he never really committed to work the 12 Steps of Recovery, which are the foundation of the healing process for addiction within AA.

The nature of this whole experience is more complicated than a teenager doing drugs and trying to get clean. He had been smoking weed for some time and had experimented with some other drugs, but when he took this ecstasy pill, something extraordinary happened. He had an Awakening. In the midst of all the chaos, he became aware of the unified field of consciousness. He was able to see the Oneness of all things. A veil had been lifted, and his perception of reality would never be the same. Initially, when we saw him two days after he had taken the drug, he was in an unusually open state, full of love and gratitude. By then, the effects of the high should have worn off, but he was still experiencing this open-hearted 'ecstasy.' He told me that he finally understood all the (esoteric) things I have shared with him over the years. Concepts of energy and vibration felt real and tangible to him then. He was especially warm and open to everyone, uncharacteristic of his more usual uncommunicative teenage disposition. The drug facilitated a powerful heart opening in him that was undeniable. In my naiveté, I did not suspect drugs. Sherman did and checked his backpack. Adaire was also concerned. Even when we became aware of him taking the drug, and his mental state became erratic and disjointed over the next week, I knew that something more was happening. His excitement about his newfound perception made him unable to rest or sleep, and he ate very little that week. He prolifically wrote lyrics to raps, and yet they were not fully cohesive, nor was his train of thought that ensued throughout that week. I do not want to relive the details of his unraveling. Let it be enough to say that by the time we arrived with him at the hospital, we felt there was no other choice than for him to be admitted. We feared that he had lost his mind, not knowing if he would ever 'come back.'

A year or so before this incident, I had a dream: Chaz and I were walking in a parking lot to get to our car. We looked down to realize that the ground was covered with water and beginning to flood. I noticed islands of dry ground that I felt we could jump across to make it to the car without getting too wet. I told him that, urging him to hurry. Just then, I looked back, and he dove head first into the shallow water. I screamed and said it was too shallow to dive. He came up out of the water, bloody and bruised, but completely unaffected by his condition, peaceful and serene. I was horrified.

I feel the dream symbolizes his fearlessness and willingness to dive into the wild, dark waters of the unknown, regardless of the consequences. I wanted to stay dry and play it safe so that I could get out of the impending flood . . . not wanting to drown in the emotion, symbolized by the water. It is not in his nature to play it safe. He rollerbladed at the age of two, and by the time he was eight, he would skate on the ramps whenever he got a chance. When he was three, riding a two-wheeler, he was so little that he would have to throw both legs to one side to jump off. He practiced backflips until he nailed them. He found joy in his body and naturally explored its limits.

This Ecstasy drama was complex and dynamic and would facilitate a whole new trajectory in his life and ours. We navigated the mind-field of fear, distrust, psychiatric meds, addiction, self-doubt, openings, revelations, recovery, psychosis, control and lack of it. This was an adventure that he called forth, and obviously on some level, so did we. Although it was one of the most harrowing experiences of my life, I now see it from the broader view. I see how it is all a part of the process, the intricate tapestry of Awakening.

Now, almost six years later, he still speaks of this transforming shift in perception as the most important experience he has ever had. He says he still has an awareness of the energetic field and the knowing that he received in his state of heightened sensitivity after the ecstasy. He says he has learned to not talk about it as much and discern with whom to share this part of himself. I would think how incredibly different his perspective of this experience was from Sherman's and mine. I don't know if he realizes how close he came to losing his mind, and I am not sure if he really cares. There truly is a thin line between what we deem sane and insane. He would teeter on the edge of that line a few more times as he continued to explore his limits and define his desires. He experienced more painful contractions, struggling to make choices that were healthy; all the while, these contractions were delivering him forward towards a clearer vision and towards experiences that would bring him closer to his True Self.

As I write, Chaz is on a new adventure, pushing his comfort zone on an Outward Bound Course for three months. He is busy sailing, scuba diving, white water rafting and kayaking in the Florida Keys, Costa Rica and Panama. He is finding his way, and I now trust that he will.

Coming to this place of trust has been my journey of

Awakening. For so long, I would live in a perceived future of what could happen to this beautiful son of mine. I was wrought with worry, seldom able to sustain present moment awareness. You would think I only had one son by my preoccupation with chronic worry for this one. I tried my best to give my attention to my other sweet boys, who were so easy going and self-sufficient that it was easy to stay obsessed with my addictive fear for my first son. Thank God they had each other.

That brings me back around to the *12 Steps to Awakening* class that Duke was offering. I decided I would check it out for myself, mostly out of curiosity, since Adaire believed so much in it, and I really did not understand what it was all about, other than there were people I knew who benefited greatly from the process, which had transformed their previously unmanageable lives. Thinking of myself as the most moderate person I knew, without an addictive bone in my body, I did not see how this would apply to me. I guess I figured I would fall into the category of codependent, but I had not made the connection to how that was an addictive pattern of thought.

This Awakening class took a less conventional approach to addiction than I was accustomed. I soon realized that my addiction was to the well-being of my son. That was what came up for me as we started filling out worksheets and exploring the broader context of addiction. I realized that my life had become unmanageable, because I was trying to control this condition that I had no control of . . . the well-being of my son. Now that is a hard one for a mother. Everything in our DNA tells us that we are responsible for the well-being of our children. To a great extent we are, when they first come into this world. I took this job of mothering very seriously and deviated from the standard, carved-out approach to parenting. I wanted to excel at doing what I felt was the very best for my sons. I questioned everything and explored different approaches when something did not seem to be working. My sons all went to Montessori schools, a more alternative approach to education. Our primary family doctor is a chiropractor. I was careful not to use pharmaceutical drugs and primarily treated any malady with homeopathy and other natural remedies. I had home births with all three sons. I copiously read books that would support me in my 'spiritual and conscious' approach to parenting. I very much considered parenting a spiritual path.

Of course, I was concerned about all of the boys' well-being, but my worry and fear for Chaz's well-being became more addictive in its nature. My life truly felt unmanageable (emotionally), because I could not control him being healthy and safe. I felt as if life would be better and all would be well, as long as he was well. This was a far cry from the Unconditional Love that I have been talking about. But this is before I really understood what that was.

The first of the 12 Steps is: *I have come to admit that I am powerless over _____ and my life has become unmanageable.* Fill in the blank with whatever your addiction is. The freedom in clarifying this addiction was that it gave it a container. I was able to see that when I was triggered by Chaz and the fear I felt for him, that I really was powerless over controlling my own addictive response. Becoming aware of it as an addiction, helped me to notice when I was getting into the danger zone of indulging in this negative thought pattern.

The second step is: *I have come to believe that a power greater than myself can restore me to sanity.*

The third step is: *I have made a decision to turn my will and my life over to the care of God as I understand 'Him.'*

The second step was easy for me. I already had a belief in a power greater than the self that was subject to such addictive thinking and suffering. I believed that this power was part of me and that it could restore me to sanity. Yet, I hadn't really thought of it that way before, thinking in terms of my addictive condition as a form of insanity. But it was, and I was powerless over it. I could not fix it. I had no control over the chronic worry and fearful thinking.

The third step makes me want to breathe a deep sigh of relief. Tingles cascade through me when I think of the surrender that this step elicits in me. Not only was I willing to turn my will and life over to the care of God, but I was also ready to turn my son over to the care of God. What a relief it was for me to let go of the illusion that I am responsible for the well-being of this child of God. When I am in this addictive pattern, I am disconnected from the truth of my son's divine nature. I forget that he has his own divine guidance that is perfect for him and his perfect unfolding.

My mother joined me on this twelve-week journey into the steps. We both benefited greatly from the process and began to feel the relief and transformations that came from this inquiry. We formed a small like-minded group from the large group, and we met at my mother's home weekly for a three-hour intensive, continuing the deep work of Recovery. We are still meeting, and it is powerful and intimate, and we are evolving rapidly as a result of our commitment and support. At this point, we have expanded beyond the format of the 12 Steps, and yet we come back to it as a touchstone to see where we are in relationship to our addictions. Primarily, our group is dealing with addictive patterns of thoughts, even more so than substance addiction. And yet, all addictions stem from thought patterns, which are often caused by the need for control. There is a saying in AA, "It isn't your drinking that is stinking, it is your thinking."

I feel that the work that I have done with the 12 Steps has been a critical springboard into a new level of awakening in this never-ending process. I began to notice when I would be triggered by a small thing that would throw me into the addictive thought pattern. I remember the day Chaz asked me for five dollars for gas and it triggered my addiction. I started thinking, "This kid is never going to get his shit together. He is terrible with money management. Even if he is working, he never has money. He will never move out and be independent. I should have taught him more about money. It is all my fault." Ugh! Painful. Ridiculous. That is the nature of addiction. The next thing you know, I am flipping out, crying, feeling guilty, frustrated and weak. He would usually join me in my pain, feeling guilty, sorry and miserable too.

So this was one of the first times I noticed myself spiraling into the addiction with the awareness of what was happening. I did not become fully unconscious, but the momentum was too strong for me to pull right out of it before it began. Nevertheless, I was able to recognize it and let him know what I realized was happening in me. As time went on, I indulged less and less, and then I came upon something that would offer me another level of support to catapult me into another awakening, allowing more freedom and joy to flood into my experience!

12

Flower Therapy

M Y FIRST EXPOSURE TO BACH Flower Essences was when I attended an event at a local wellness center. Various practitioners were giving fifteen-minute sessions so that you could get a sampling of what they had to offer. I sat with a woman who was an Intuitive and quickly and furiously told her my dilemma with my son. This was not long after he had been hospitalized and after several months of sobriety and attending AA meetings, he was beginning to get antsy and depressed. He wanted to get out and be a part of the 'normal' teenage social life again. I can't remember much of what she said, other than to buy a bottle of Rescue Remedy, which is a blend of five Bach Flower Essences, and give it to him twice a day. She told me to give it to the rest of the family as well, but only once per day, because we all had been impacted by the shock of the recent event, and we would all benefit from this remedy. She said I should expect to notice a difference within two weeks.

I went out to buy the remedy the very next day at the local health-food store. Just as she said, within two weeks I noticed a huge shift. Chaz was happy, dancing and singing around the house. He even invited a friend to come over and hang out with the family, something he rarely did. I was impressed. Within time, I forgot about the remedy and life went on with its ups and downs.

It would be a couple of years later when I would think about the magical flower essences again. Out of the blue, I decided to look up information about them online. I started to read about the thirty-eight different remedies made by the Bach Flower company. I was fascinated. There were two remedies in particular that I decided I needed to purchase right away. One was Red Chestnut, which is to help those of us who worry about loved ones. That one had my name written all over it. The other was Walnut, for those who are going through a life transition. It also helps to protect us from outside influences, so that we can move forward with what we know we want to do. Of course, I thought this would be perfect for Chaz, who was preparing to go off for ten months to serve in AmeriCorps, a US-based community service program.

I decided that I wanted to find out more about these mysterious remedies, and I was able to find one book in our library system, which I ordered to be delivered to a branch close to me. When I started to read the information within the book, and the quotes from the creator of the flower essences, Dr. Edward Bach, I felt this resonance that sent those tingly goose bumps running through my body. I was fascinated and riveted by the whole philosophy and creation of this vibrational healing modality. I was shocked that it had taken me so long to find it. I had been using homeopathic remedies with my children since they were infants, which is also a form of vibrational medicine. I had taken a workshop on homeopathy many years before and had my own kit of remedies, feeling confident that even if I chose the wrong remedy, that it was safe and benign, without side effects. This natural approach to health appealed to me very much, and I had first-hand experience of their efficacy.

I became totally absorbed with studying these healing flowers and the different ways in which they were able to support the emotional and mental well-being of those who used them. As I read the indications for each essence, I made notes on which ones would help various people I knew. I became so excited about the possibilities of helping others to feel more balance, freedom and joy in their lives that I wanted to know all I could about this simple yet profound modality for healing.

Bach Flower Essences are taken internally in the form of liquid drops or a spray that can be added to water or any drink. They are similar to homeopathic remedies but are more stable in their constitution, so there is no concern about taking it with food, caffeine, alcohol, etc., which in homeopathy will deactivate the effectiveness of the remedy. The flowers essences treat the emotional and mental conditions, not the physical body. Dr. Bach was a traditional family doctor, an emergency room physician, then a homeopathic doctor and researcher, after which he was inspired to create a purer form of healing and discovered the flower essences. By the time he came upon this new cutting-edge approach to healing, he was passionate about going to the core cause of disease, which he believed stemmed from the state of mind, indicated by our emotions. The remedies treated conditions such as anxiety, fear, terror, shock, indecision, depression, despair, feeling overwhelmed, exhaustion from overwork, stress, over-enthusiasm, worry, perfectionism, impatience, intolerance of others, resentment, self-pity and so on. He believed that when you heal the emotional condition, then the physical manifestations of disease will heal and be cured. He also felt it was best to take the remedies before the physical conditions appeared to maintain both a healthy state of mind and body.

I felt completely in agreement with his philosophy and was eager to put the flowers to the test. I understood that they were safe for anyone to use because of the vibrational nature of the remedies that did not contain any actual substance of the flowers, but just the vibrational essence of them, which is stabilized in water and preserved with brandy. I was eager to take a mix of the remedies myself as well as offer consultations to friends and family to do the same, if they were interested. I bought several books, including a workbook, and learned the indications for each flower essence, inside and out. Eventually and organically, I began to consult anyone who desired to explore this avenue of healing.

I feel so blessed and so much joy when I am able to offer something that is helpful and even transformational to another. The perfection of Flowers becoming an approach to healing and spiritual evolvement for me was truly magical. I have been painting the essence of flowers a great deal of my life! My home and shop are filled with the essence of flowers and nature in the form of big, bold, colorful paintings. Some would describe my work as inspired by Georgia O'Keeffe, especially her floral images. My art is less literal and comes from a deep place within my heart, not from the visual interpretation of the flower, but from the visceral awareness of the oneness between nature and the divine nature of humanity.

What I love most about the Flower Therapy is the spiritual basis that is at its very foundation. This quote from Dr. Edward Bach is what got me hooked:

> *The action of these Remedies is to raise our vibrations and open up our channels for the reception of our Spiritual Self; to flood our natures with the particular virtue we need, and wash out from us the fault which is causing harm. They are able, like beautiful music or any glorious uplifting thing, which gives us inspiration, to raise our very natures, and bring us nearer to our souls, and by that very act bring us peace and relieve our sufferings. They cure, not by attacking disease, but by flooding our bodies with the beautiful vibrations of our Higher Nature, in the presence of whom disease melts away as snow in the sunshine. (pg.13) Illustrated Handbook of the Bach Flower Remedies by Philip M. Chancellor*

When I read this, I knew this would be part of my spiritual path. There are many paths to vibrational healing; this one was tailor-made for me. It resonated with my desire to avoid toxic substances for the purpose of healing, which was more common within western pharmaceuticals. It spoke to my love of nature and specifically my connection to flowers, as they were inspired to come forth in my artwork. It addressed my deep longing to be connected to my True Self, the Divine Source, offering a tangible approach to removing the blocks that keep us from this connection. The Flowers felt like Divine Guidance, offering yet another creative way to heal our discord so that we may know our brilliance and perfection once more. To live from this place of knowing is by far the greatest gift we can receive and give the world. For when we live our lives from this awareness, all manner of beauty and love is possible. Transformation of all that is not Love is imminent.

After several months of taking a mix of several different remedies, I began to feel the shifts. For me, it was gradual and somewhat subtle, and yet very profound. For some, it is immediate and dramatic. The Red Chestnut that I was taking for the chronic worry I felt for my son and his well-being, as I recognized as my addictive thought pattern, worked miracles on me. I could barely believe that I was finally feeling relief from this painful condition I had been living with for so long. I figured that some of the relief was from the fact that he was not living in the house, and so there was less opportunity to be triggered, and yet I noticed each time I saw him or spoke to him during this past year that my responses and inner feelings were less and less attached. It is hard to explain, but essentially I am not worrying about him for the first time in his life. I feel more trust in his well-being and in his own connection to Divine Guidance. I cannot begin to tell you what a relief that is to me! I now have access to a reservoir of joy that I had rarely felt before. The incredible thing is that the conditions of life did not need to change for me to feel this freedom. When the change comes from within, then the conditions begin to reflect the inner shift. It is called living from the inside out!

Another issue that I had been struggling with, since before I can remember, is the phobia of public speaking. It has been a real hindrance for me to live with this debilitating fear that ravishes my body with miserable symptoms that the fear elicits. Mostly, I have avoided public speaking at all costs and had made that part of my identity. Other than my challenges with

Chaz, it is the only other issue that brought me to a therapist for help. I felt paralyzed by this phobia, and I really wanted to be able to speak up and out when I had something to share, no matter what the size of the group. I wanted to feel fearless.

For several months, I took the remedy Mimulus, which is for fear of a known thing. After about six months, I was asked to speak to a group about the Bach Flowers. The fact that I said yes was the miracle that made me aware that the flowers were working for me. Since then, I have done several other talks, and while the sensation of adrenaline rushing has not gone away, I am feeling less paralyzed by it and have even felt excitement about having the opportunity to practice speaking. I have always had a lot to say but invariably held back in groups because of this issue. I am feeling some freedom in that area as well.

The shifts that people were experiencing as a result of taking the flowers were proof enough to me of their efficacy. Not only was I undergoing profound healing and transformation in my own vibrational body, but I was also discovering a whole new direction in my own life purpose. While it felt magical and exciting, it also felt organic and natural and ordained for me to begin this vocation of counseling through Bach Therapy.

At the same time, I feel an awareness that it is just the beginning of sharing and serving the Divine in this new way, and I am open and eager to see what new magical avenues will be revealed to me. My art has been a part of that sharing allowing Divine Energy to flow through me and out of me. My boutique/gallery, Utopia, has offered me a venue for the exchange of energy and goods as well as a beautiful environment primed for meaningful connection that goes beyond the interaction of selling clothes or art. It is truly my joy-place more than my workplace. It is creative and alive with the energy of my art and the artistic expression of each designer I showcase.

Mothering has been a powerful way for the Divine to live on through my willingness to give birth and nurture the lives of my sons. I have received Divine love through them in a way that has surpassed all understanding and has rendered me helpless to control the love that floods into and through me as a result of this gift. My heart has felt ripped open when I have resisted the powerful flow of my own desires, leaving me raw and ravaged, only to find out that, in my surrender, I am delivered to the greatest joy and the deepest love that I have ever known. Each blessed contraction delivers me to the Divine, to knowing the Divine in All that Is.

13

UNITY

" DIVINE LOVE BLESSES AND MULTIPLIES all that I have, all that I give and all that I receive, and I am grateful." This is one of the statements I love that we say every Sunday morning at Unity Church of Charleston, a lovey oasis where like-minded people gather to experience the connection with each other and the energy of the space held by our openhearted minister, Ed Kosak. My way of thinking and connecting to the Divine is definitely not mainstream. It does not fit into the traditional concepts of most religions, and so it was wonderful to find a spiritual community that offers more of the principles of thought that resonate with mine.

I had occasionally dropped into Unity over the years to participate in a workshop or see a guest speaker. It is there where I was first introduced to Byron Katie in person. Years ago, Unity brought Neale Donald Walsh, author of

Conversations with God, to Charleston. This is before I was regularly attending. Since I work in Utopia on Fridays and Saturdays, I always loved that on Sundays I could just be at home or go to the beach and be with God in the way I loved most . . . in nature. My mother had become a member of Unity, and I always liked the message and the perspective but never felt the need to go to any church, until one particular day.

It had been a difficult Saturday night. I do not remember any details, thank goodness, other than I think that there was an intense argument between Sherman and Chaz, because Chaz was miserable that Sunday morning. The tension in the house was thick and frequently was during this time of navigating Chaz's adolescence and the precarious choices he made.

I decided to take the three boys to church, so I piled them in the car and dragged them to Unity. In church, Chaz sat next to me with his body slouched over his lap and his head in his hands. The pain in his being was palpable. I was definitely not feeling the enlightened state of Unconditional Love at that time. I was feeling his pain and my pain and barely could decipher the difference between the two. I needed help. I felt like I was drowning in the confusion and stress of feeling responsible for this child's welfare and having no idea how to guide him. Now I realize that it is impossible to guide someone from a place of disconnection. As a matter of fact, I had asked Abraham, in person at a workshop, how to support our children on their path, and Abraham said, amongst other things, "It is only ever from a place of disconnection that you are ever trying to guide someone." Wow! It was five years later when I was re-listening to the recording of that workshop that I actually *heard* that statement and got it. I realize that we are only ready to hear something when we are ripe to hear it..

What that means to me is that we try to guide when we think that there is something wrong, and therefore, we are perceiving from a place of lack, fear and worry. Real influence comes when we are in alignment with Source, and when we are, we can perceive through the eyes of Source who sees the perfection in all things. Abraham suggests that we *soothe* another into alignment. This requires a certain amount of inner alignment within yourself. This allows you to see the beauty, perfection and well-being in another. When in this state, when you focus on another, your very presence soothes them into alignment and then they have access to their own unique inner guidance.

In that same encounter that was recorded, March 3, 2016 in Asheville, NC, Abraham also said:

> *"We know your well-being and never deviate from that. That is what makes us of advantage to you and that is what will make you of advantage to your children too: to practice so well your thoughts of their well-being; to practice so well your trust in the true nature of their being; to practice so well your awareness of what their life has caused them to want and flow with their well-being. Do not let yourself be drawn into any of the drama that there may be, and you will find yourself offering the benefit to your children that Abraham offers you."*

This workshop was recorded when Chaz was only thirteen years old. Little did I know the drama that would ensue or how challenging it would be for me to follow this advice. Yet, the seed had been planted.

101

Another statement we often say and affirm in Unity that reflects this principle is, "You are whole, perfect, healthy and free, even when the facts of your life, your human condition, may indicate otherwise." Abraham speaks of the healing abilities of Jesus Christ in a way that perfectly describes this. When Jesus was approached by those who begged to be healed, and they came to Him dripping in their illnesses, He saw them as whole, perfect, healthy and free. He saw them as God sees them, knowing their well-being completely. This is what healed them. His aligned influence was powerful.

"More powerful is one that is in alignment than a million that are not," says Abraham.

That day at Unity, I was definitely not in alignment, and yet I knew enough to summon the energy to bring us all to this intentional gathering. Sitting there in the murky muck of pain, an angel glided into our midst. She was a beautiful, tall, young woman wearing denim overalls with long wavy red hair pulled back from her face in a tight ponytail. She took Chaz by the hand and pulled him out of his seat and escorted him to the back rooms of the church where the youth gathered during services. She was one of the YOU (Youth of Unity) facilitators. Elizabeth Watson was a bright light that flitted and fired through Unity. A few years later, she made her transition into the non-physical realms, offering her divine service as an angel in heaven. That day, she was our angel on earth, and I doubt if he had resisted if she would have taken no for an answer.

I remember sitting there in church hearing words spoken through Ed, through songs sung, that resonated with the pain I was feeling, attempting to soothe me and to connect to the truth of who I am, who my son is. Tears rolled down my face as I absorbed the love, acceptance and compassion that seemed to emanate from the space.

The miracle happened when I saw my son come into the sanctuary at the end of service holding an angel card in his hand with a big smile on his face. He was standing up straight, and light beamed from his being. He exclaimed the perfection of the words that were contained on his card that spoke to the dilemma he was facing and offered a solution to his approach. He was able to open up and share his pain with the group, and he felt relief. He experienced the Grace that would weave its way through his life for years to come.

At that moment, I committed to coming to Unity every Sunday. I realized that I needed help. I needed a like-minded spiritual community that could support me in supporting my son through this minefield of adolescence. Not to mention I had two other lovely sons that would have the advantage of growing up in this loving and diverse environment. It was a sweet moment of awareness, and I was filled with gratitude. While God for me is everywhere and in all moments, I finally understood some of the main reasons why a lot of people go to church. It isn't necessarily to *find* God. It is to be with others who are focusing on God at the same time together. It is about spiritual community. It is about holding an intention collectively for the higher good.

While I have come to cultivate my awareness of nonphysical guidance and support, we all need people and community to give us strength and love in a tangible way. Churches, spiritual communities and organizations that offer community and fellowship are an invaluable part of our society in offering support to those who desire and need it. The challenge is to find the one that is best for you, the one that feels right and resonates with your inner being. I love that there are so many options available in the world. The paths to God are as varied and as diverse as the many humans who live on this earth. I love being part of a spiritual community that honors these many paths and is able to see the beauty in all of them. It is my belief that no matter what path is chosen, we all end up at the same place eventually, reunited with our Divine Source. This may happen in flashes of brilliant awakenings throughout a lifetime, but without a doubt, it will inevitably happen when we leave our dense, physical reality and re-emerge with the pure positive energy from which we all came.

14

Divine Guidance and Spirit Guides

C ULTIVATING A CONNECTION WITH YOUR divine guidance is an exciting and magical journey. Yesterday, as I was walking in my beloved park, I was feeling heavy. The weather has been gloomy for a few days, and business has been slow in the shop. It is the beginning of March, and we are all ready for spring to come, tired of the shorter and colder days. I was trying my best to stay positive but was feeling the need for a boost from my non-physical friends. I was grateful that the weather was finally warmer so that I could walk. I wanted a tangible awareness of the Guidance that I knew was with me but seems elusive at times. I asked for a sign to let me know I was not alone.

I continued to walk, open to the infinite possibilities that Source might show me its divine presence in an extraordinary way. The sun was coming out from behind the clouds, warming me and coaxing me to take off my jacket. Within about five or ten minutes, I looked up into the sky to see a few birds that looked like hawks fly above me and over the lake next to my path. They began to circle overhead, and as I looked more closely, I noticed that one of the birds was a bald eagle! All but the eagle flew away out of my sight, and for several more minutes, the eagle continued circling in flight above me. Wow! If that is not a direct sign for the Divine, I don't know what is. And, of course, it was tailor-made for me since the eagle has become an important spiritual symbol of Awakening for me. I rarely see eagles. It has been maybe three times now since my first dramatic eagle sighting. Never has it been as dramatic as that first time. They have been further away, mostly in flight. Once, one perched on the top branch of a very tall tree. Of course, the rareness of seeing my majestic spirit animal makes it all the more magical when I do.

I am filled with gratitude for the immediate response, and I feel a deep sense of comfort and joy to be aware of this benevolent force. I am learning to become more and more intimate with Divine Source Energy, and this past year, I have begun to consciously connect to the more personal aspect of the Divine that I have always thought of as God...the All that Is. Now, I have connected with spirit guides and enjoy this new way of aligning with Source. I have become aware of two guides that are with me often. I had a psychic reading that first let me know the nature of these guides. My life guide was described as a beautiful, tall dark male with angular features. As my life guide, he is always present and has been for my whole life. The psychic said that I draw him to me when I am in a state of gratitude.

I also have a female guide who is very much a part of my work with the Bach Flowers, and she wanted me to figure out her name on my own. I was given a few hints, but was encouraged to go into meditation and ask for her to reveal her name to me directly. When I did this, I closed my eyes and saw a flower in my mind's eye. I was already given the hint that her name was one of the Bach flowers and that it had three syllables. I asked her if I should look it up online. I felt a yes answer, so I looked at the Bach Flower pictures until I saw the flower that was exactly like the one in my inner vision. It was Cerato, a blue five-petalled flower. I knew that this was her name and felt the confirmation of this by the cascading tingles that I feel when truth is revealed or when I sense the presence of my Divine guidance.

The cool thing is that the flower essence Cerato is about trusting your intuition, your inner guidance. That is why she would not just give her name to the psychic. She wants me to develop my own inner trust. I began to take the remedy as a consistent part of my personal Bach Therapy. I feel that so much of my work with the flower essences has been about cultivating this inner trust and connecting with the Divine realm in a personal way. I have come to understand that, for both myself and others, my intuitive abilities are just as valuable in choosing the best mix of remedies as studying the qualities of the essences. The experience of working with the Flowers has been a divine path, which has led me to develop my intuition and to gain even more confidence in that intuitive knowing. I love how the Universe creatively offers us a plethora of ways to connect more deeply with our purpose and our true nature.

In a world of tangible reality, it is difficult at times to trust in the unseen. And yet, it is the unseen that sometimes seems more real than what is right in front of us. Think about it. Our feelings are an intangible manifestation of our thoughts. Our thoughts themselves can take us into a world that is far from the reality right in front of us. I could be thinking about the past in great detail while sitting in the midst of a dinner party, totally disconnected from the experience that we consider real. Abraham talks about how our practiced thoughts create our beliefs, and our practiced beliefs create our reality. The majority of the time, most people are creating their reality by observing what is, and thus recreating more of the same, which isn't very creative. We were not meant to be facers of reality but creators of reality. So essentially, real is only real because we have practiced it into reality collectively, over time and usually unconsciously.

So what does it really mean to trust in your Self, your Inner Being, your intuition or inner guidance? It is cultivating your awareness of how you feel. It is listening to this inner guidance system that lets us know when we are lined up with Source. To the degree that I feel bad or good, and all those various feelings that are felt on this emotional scale, is the degree that I am in alignment or not with the nonphysical part of me, which is aware of its Oneness with Source energy.

For some, it is developing their clairvoyance and the other 'clairs', such as clairaudience, clairsentience, and claircognizance, along with other intuitive, non-physical, psychic senses. I have come to understand that you do not necessarily have to be born with this gift but can actually develop it. Many of us already have the intuitive ability to sense, see or hear what is not in the realm of tangible reality, and we don't even realize it. I noticed that when my grandparents passed away, I could smell them occasionally. Out of the blue, I would smell my grandpa's cologne. I remember once smelling my grandmother's perfume in the car, while I was driving alone. It was so pungent and clear to me that it was her that I just *had* to acknowledge her presence. The scent would go as quickly and mysteriously as it had appeared, which is not exactly the nature of strong smells that tend to linger.

I also have the capacity to sense energy on a visceral level and think that I could develop that sense more, if I could know how to keep myself from being swept away or consumed by the many energies around me. I have felt challenged in doing that right here in the tangible world. Although, I have gotten better since I started taking a flower essence to help with that. I have never been able to 'see' and am fascinated by those who do. This is what I would typically think of when I think of a psychic—one who sees and hears beyond the veil of our physical reality.

I am not quite sure how much I want to develop these skills. Mostly I want to feel connected to my Divine Self, to feel connected to the whole. I want to feel free, joyful and alive. I want to experience this physical world, while also being aware of the nonphysical. I am enthralled by the mystery of the world of spirit and love the magical ways in which it infuses itself into my experience. The more awake I become to these subtle energies, the more aligned I feel and the more joy and ease I experience in my life. Through this process, I enrich the manifested reality of my life and the lives of those I share this life with. I love knowing that there are angels, guides and loved ones that are looking out for me, supporting me each step of the way. This belief is strong, and I feel that I have received confirmation of this truth; but what is most important, is how it makes me *feel* to believe in what I do. The feelings of well-being and comfort and love let me know that I am on the right track. I am aligned with Source. I am aligned with my Inner Being.

I am so grateful for this guidance. We all have it. All we need to do is tune in to it, make it a priority, and we will feel the well-being and love pour in. Awakening is a practice, an intention, and it is cultivated over time. There are few of us that experience spontaneous Awakening. Most of us do not sustain the full Awakening all the time but are transformed in a way that allows for the practice to begin and for Awakening to evolve. When there is the desire to be free of the suffering that the human mind inflicts, Awakening is the path to freedom from this state. When we recognize our desire, then so does the Universe, and the Universe responds. Divine Guidance is always available. The question is, are you asking and then are you listening, seeing and receiving what you have asked for?

15

BODY AND BREATH

I LOVE NIA. IT IS A "sensory-based movement practice" with a mix of dance styles, martial arts and yoga. It is therapeutic and aerobic and freeing. I started taking classes from a beautiful, sensual, dynamic woman, Lisa Geddings, in Charleston many years ago. Her personal experience with Nia was a deep releasing of old fears and inhibitions that led her on a journey of self-love and service, supporting the liberation of others. She had a therapy practice that incorporated movement therapy. I have never been much of a fan of working out with weights and aerobic exercise. I tried, but I couldn't seem to stick with it for very long, but I loved taking Nia classes with Lisa. It was a spiritual experience, and like yoga, it engaged, healed and expressed the connection between body and mind and spirit.

Eventually, she moved out of town, and several years later,

made her transition after a sudden and rapid bout with cancer. I like to think of these beautiful women that I have known, who seem to have left our world too soon and too young, as angelic beings. Perhaps their spirits were so expansive and fearless that they were called to a higher purpose that required them to merge back into the nonphysical realm. Each one has left an indelible mark on those who knew and loved them.

I began taking Nia classes with some other wonderful teachers at Spirit Moves, a dance studio nearby. My dear friend Alex and I went weekly for our Nia fix, and one fated day, it seemed the schedule had changed, and instead of Nia, there was going to be a Qigong class. I was disappointed, but one of the women present suggested that we try it out. She thought we would enjoy it. The teacher was a very young, lovely woman with a low, raspy voice. She introduced herself as Hanna. Little did I know what we were in for that day!

She began the class with this tapping technique: with fists closed we tapped on our lower abdomen or pelvis area. We stood in a circle, and each of us alternately counted in tens around the circle. I think that it may have been five hundred taps before we went on to the next phase. As the class progressed, there were points when we were holding a challenging posture for ten to fifteen minutes. Her voice of encouragement was strong and powerful, and her eyes were full of compassion and love. She would say things like, "You are not your body; your body is yours. You can do this!" She continued with intensity, holding us up with her words and her spirit. I remember tears rolling down my eyes and sweat dripping down my sides as we held the 'eagle' stance for what seemed like an eternity. I had taken a series of Qigong classes years before, and this did not resemble anything I remembered. It was all very new and intense and exhilarating. We did some type of breathing process at the end of the class, which sent me floating into another dimension. I was a complete soggy mess by the end, but something magical had happened during those two or more hours. I felt a lightness and a feeling of being unhinged and liberated from the deep-seated, painful, solid blocks of energy that had been calcifying within my being. This was during the time when I felt so challenged by the tension and uncertainty of the roller coaster ride with my son Chaz.

During the class, I was looking at how this beautiful, young, powerful woman had more presence than most women twice her age and thought, "I know her. Where do I know her from?" Her voice seemed so familiar. I kept trying to remember what she said her name was. And then all of a sudden it hit me. All the pieces of the puzzle fell into place. I walked up to her at the end of the class, and I said to her, "I know you. You are Hanna, Charlie's daughter." Charlie was my first midwife, the one who attended Chaz's birth sixteen or so years before. She said, "I know. You are Beki." The last time I saw Hanna she was four or five years old! The crazy thing is that she remembered me! We embraced and wept. It was like a homecoming, but beyond our recognition of this life experience; it felt like we had reconnected from lifetimes of knowing.

I was blown away by her wisdom and intensity of presence. At one point during the class, she held her gaze on each one of us, looking deep into our souls with this unflinching, loving energy that surpassed inhibition and inspired opening and ease, rather than that squirming discomfort that this type of intimacy often elicits. Maybe it was me and my willingness to be seen, maybe it was her and her magical ability to be intense and balanced in lightness at the same time. I am not quite sure, but my wise friend Alex felt something similar. We were both floored by the experience and realized that we had stumbled upon a gem of an opportunity, and we did not miss one of her classes after that. I had a feeling that she would not be in Charleston long, for her gift was way beyond what could be contained or appreciated in this small venue. Her class was much more of a workshop than a class, and her offering was truly a gift.

She told me later that the technique she was offering was a fusion of qigong and Don Yoga, which is a type of yoga from Korea. Hanna and I easily became friends. My children adored her, and we all embraced her as part of our family. As I predicted, she was not with us long before she got a position working with Qi Revolution, an organization that teaches Qigong and Food Healing to large gatherings of up to one thousand people at a time, over four-day long workshops.

She came to town several months after Chaz had been hospitalized for the drug-induced psychosis and offered to do a private session with me in my home. I gratefully accepted, and she 'tapped' me back into the world. I felt that my inner flame had gone out. I was so utterly depleted and disconnected from my Source. It must have been close to three hours, and soon I could begin to feel my blood warming and life entering my shell once again. It really felt like she was helping me to stoke my inner fire. As the fire began to take, I could feel some strength slowly seep back into my being. I realized that I needed to be very careful and protective of this new flame, to make sure a gust of wind did not blow it out. During that traumatic time, I had been unable to make any decisions; I felt weak and listless, afraid and incapable. I had lost my awareness to my connection to the Divine Guidance that offeres all solutions. I did not seem to have access to this inner knowing and went outside myself for the answers.

I gingerly reentered my life after this powerful reawakening and reigniting, fiercely protecting the me that I had lost. I remembered what I learned seventeen years before—when Chaz was a baby—that I needed to tend to my own well-being before I could take care of anyone else. I needed to come first, or I would have nothing to offer.

I am eternally grateful for Hanna's gift to me. Her offering is unique and precious and very dynamic. I feel she will have a significant impact on raising the vibration of this planet. As a consequence of our work together, I decided to attend the Qi Revolution workshop, which I have now done three times. It was really a powerful experience, especially the first time. It is another amazing tool for accessing our divine nature. Qigong, for me, is really about becoming aware and in tune with the vibrational energy field around us and harnessing it through movements with our arms and hands, consciously breathing in rhythm with the forms. Qi stands for the energy in everything, the life force that every person and thing has. Cultivating your awareness of your Qi, using the practice of qigong, is another way to awaken to the subtle energy that is not all that subtle when you tune into it. This workshop, led by a dynamic and inspired teacher, Jeff Primack, includes not only lessons in qigong forms, but also food healing classes and breathing techniques that can send you floating into orbit without losing your mind.

The first time I experienced the healing circle using the nine-breath method, created by Jeff, I was so blown away. I felt that I had literally left my body and had merged with the energy vibrating throughout the universe. I was with two friends who flanked me during this process. There were hundreds of people there, and we are all holding hands. Alex said afterward that she had to look down at my hand to see if I was still there, because she could feel me 'go.' I was in such an altered state that my friends practically had to carry me out. My eyes were blurry. It was beautiful and moving and undoubtedly another step in my evolving journey of Awakening.

16

Becoming

I DID NOT COME HERE TO be what I was before I came. I did not come here to be enlightened. I did not come to be a Buddha or a Christ or even a Byron Katie. I smile as I write this. I came forth into the physical realm of duality so that I could immerse myself in the illusion of separateness for the experience of remembering and *becoming* awakened to what I already am. I came for the becoming. I came for my unique path to Awakening. Without this illusion, there is no experience. I came for the journey, the ride, the adventure. I came to know once again the Ultimate Reality, the true nature of my being. I did not know how that would evolve, how it would play out in the rocky and mountainous terrain of emotions and duality, but I trusted that all would work out in the end, and I would reemerge into the wholeness of who I am. I knew that when I released this compelling and mesmerizing experience, leaving the physical body, that I would regain full awareness of the true nature of All that Is. I willingly and eagerly chose this adventure, knowing that it would offer the environment that would allow for the expansion that would benefit All that Is.

My fascination and love of God became the theme of this life experience. My desire was to know and understand the connection between the tangible world and the world of spirit and how they interrelated with each other. I yearned to feel this connection, and through the experiences of loss, disconnection, fear, pain and illness that I myself felt or witnessed in others, my yearning grew. I wanted to know how to be free from this cycle of pain and pleasure, which seemed to feed each other in a web of nourishment and self-sabotage. Consuming my share of personal pain and feeling the pain of others, gave birth to the desire for freedom and untouchable joy that propelled me on my quest for Spiritual Awakening.

Whether we know it or not, I believe that we are all on this voyage that ultimately leads to our Awakening. For some, it will happen here on earth, gradually or instantaneously. For others, the culmination of their expansion will occur at the moment of their 'death'. Some will be oblivious to the gift of their presence on this earth and the way in which their own mired experiences may be giving rise to a host of strong desires that offer the most magnificent expansion of all. All of life benefits from all of life. The contrasting experiences form the powerful trajectory we knew would give us the expansion we All desired. We cannot begin to see from our human point of view, the intricate tapestry of life and how it is all woven into a grand design of utter perfection and unfathomable beauty. Yet even in its vastness, we can taste it and sense it and get glorious glimpses of it, and in moments of sheer joy, feel the pure, blessed ecstasy of it.

When we become entangled in the human perspective, devoid of any awareness of our True Divine nature, then it can all seem like a jumbled mess of some seriously sad, tragic and insane conditions. It can seem like we are victims of fate, or genetics, or a time period, lucky or unlucky, based on circumstances completely out of our control. This dynamic and colorful illusion seems so real, so solid, so true, and yet it is our *own* divine creation that is evolving and changes with the changing thoughts of all who inhabit this planet. If we could cultivate the Eagle's point of view, one that sees from the perspective of the heavens and looks down with razor-sharp vision on the whole, unencumbered by the details that have distracted us from the beauty that is happening right in our midst, then we could begin to experience the freedom that I know I came forth to feel! Then and only then, once my broad vision is clear and my alignment with Source is solid, will I focus on the details for the sheer delight of it. I will mold the intricate details of my life with conscious, steady hands and heart, always aware of my connection with Source, allowing myself to be guided by those who see the whole picture clearly. I will marry the physical world of my earthly dwelling with the Divine world of my Spirit. I will dance the story being told through me, by me. I will paint the emotions of humanity and the celestial visions beyond my sight. I will speak with my heart and make love with my soul. I will feed the minds of my children as we eat the nectar from the earth. I will offer flowers in the form of color on canvas and contained within bottles as vibrations to consume. I will drink in nature and breathe out gratitude.

My life is a work of art—a tapestry that is entwined with the billions and trillions of other life forms that really are, in essence, just One. Not only is there just one God. There is only One, and all that seems separate from that One, is not. But oh, what fun it is to dive into this illusion of duality with such delicious diversity. It is a grand adventure, and it is unending and ever-changing.

Awakening is the consciousness that perceives the wholeness of all of life and revels in the illusion of separateness. Awakening gives rise to Love that is beyond conditions, that knows itself and all else as Love. The awakened mind resists nothing and loves what is, right here, right now . . . perfect.

17

SPIRITUAL PRACTICE

A SPIRITUAL PRACTICE IS A TANGIBLE process in which we are able to practice and cultivate our connection with God. I think that each of us benefits from different methods that will enable this awareness to develop. Thank goodness there is an abundance of ways to practice ourselves into connection.

I would have to say that my first spiritual practice was painting. It has been a profound way for me to 'plug in' to this Divine Energy. I was not aware of it being a spiritual practice until much later. Yoga definitely was another practice that allowed me a beautiful alignment with the Divine. Ironically, the physical practice of holding asanas (postures) and breathing with intention ushered me into the awareness of higher vibrational frequencies of the non-physical dimension.

In 1999, I decided to join my sisters Sarah and Joanna,

my mother and a couple more friends on a spiritual journey with Siddha Yoga for an Intensive Retreat in California. Siddha Yoga is a practice of chanting and meditation, led by the beautiful, brown-skinned Indian woman Guru, Gurumayi Chidvilasananda. The spiritual practice of chanting is particularly potent when experienced in a group. This gathering had around a thousand attendees, along with thousands more tuning in on live satellite. I went to the Intensive with the intention of shifting into a place of deep joy that was untouchable, without cause. Now, I would describe that as Unconditional Joy and Unconditional Love.

I had never been personally drawn to the concept of a guru, and yet knew very little about this ancient tradition. Sarah had declared herself a devotee of Gurumayi a few years before, and I was completely open to learning more about Siddha yoga. I went to the ashram when visiting Sarah in Oakland, CA. I loved the chanting and felt an immediate resonance with the devotional frequency of the music. The long meditations were more challenging for me, but I still liked it and wanted to develop my ability to sit and meditate. There was a video presentation of the Guru, which was my first introduction to her. I was struck by her beauty and her youth. My image of a guru was always an old Indian man in robes, or less, not unlike the persona of Mahatma Gandhi. I do not remember much of what she said, but I do remember feeling mesmerized by her energy and the tone of her voice.

My mother quickly embraced Gurumayi as her guru after she went to a smaller Intensive and did Dharshan with her, where she went up to her directly in a line of devotees and bowed at her feet. This was shortly after my mother was diagnosed with breast cancer. Gurumayi's advice to Mom was to do Japa, which meant to repeat the mantra, "Om Namah Shivaya," the main Siddha Yoga chant.

When you go to an Intensive, it is customary that all present will receive 'Shaktipat' from the Guru. It is more than a blessing. It is an infusion of energy from the spiritual master to the seeker, which brings about an awakening of the seeker's own inherent spiritual power, called Kundalini. Devotees will often share their Shaktipat stories. The experiences can be dramatic and theatrical, subtle or mystical. All of them were quite fascinating to me, and while I still was uncertain of the idea of becoming a devotee, I was very comfortable with the philosophy of this path and even more so as I began to study the literature. For me, what resonated was recognizing the Divine as being within us and that we all are capable of Awakening. The master serves as an example and an earthly teacher to guide us on our journey to Spiritual Awakening.

The Intensive *was* intense and wonderful, full of love and peace and lots and lots of people with a common intention. What a powerful vortex it created—and how amazing it felt to be a part of it! Awaiting the arrival of the Guru, had all of us full of anticipation and expectation. I did not know what to expect, feeling the star-struck energy of devotees all around me. As Gurumayi entered the room, all went silent, and she walked down a long aisle between the sea of people seated on the ground. She wore orange robes and seemed to glide through the room. The thought that struck me as I saw her small female, brown figure was, "That could be me." The sensation of familiarity with her, and the feeling of identifying with her, moved me deeply. As a woman of color living in a predominantly white culture where many of the teachers and authors of new thought spirituality are white, it was quite mind-blowing to be in a room where this small brown woman, not much older than myself, was literally being worshiped by hundreds and thousands of people of all races. That was a powerful message for me. I am sure each person has their own unique experiences and epiphanies during such an intentional and spirit-filled gathering. I believe that this simple act of identifying with the Guru was a key message for me. I feel it helped me to own my inner connection to the Divine. Identifying with this fiercely revered Guru, helped me believe in the infinite possibilities that reside within me, too.

The sitting meditations, after the ecstatic chants, were the most challenging, lasting about an hour, which felt very long at the time. I squirmed and ached and would settle in for a while, then squirmed some more, hoping not to distract my neighbor too much. Needless to say, there was not much room to stretch out. The chanting was fabulous—particularly the last chant of the three days. Narayana was the name of the chant. Gurumayi led all chants and watching her was sublime. She was full of the energy of Love, with her heart full and open and blissful. The essence of all the chants are about praising God—chanting the many names of God. Not understanding the words of the sacred Sanskrit mantras works very well for me, because it takes me out of my head and into my heart and the essence of the practice, which is to connect with the Divine within one's self and within everyone else.

The chants start really slow and build in speed and intensity gradually over forty minutes or so. It was the case with the Narayana chant, and by the end, I was in a state of full-blown joy, complete and utter ecstasy. I could barely contain myself, and I was not alone. The room was lit with the Shakti of the Divine, and spontaneously, a group of us began to dance. Soon the dance grew like wild fire around us in a synchronized spiraling, chanting, whirling frenzy. Nothing could be more delicious than this. A fire was truly lit within me, and this opening of my Kundalini, this inner flame of divine light, was another Awakening, propelling me on my path . . . my path to remembering and re-knowing my Oneness with God.

For a while, I practiced the Siddha Yoga chanting and meditation rituals and loved it. Eventually, Mom and I found a small local chapter that met every Sunday at someone's home, and we were able to chant in a group, which I feel is an important aspect of the chanting ritual. It simply is not as effective for me to chant solo. When I would go to New York on a buying trip for my shop, I would go to the Saturday night Satsang at the Siddha Yoga center right in the city. They would have a large group, and the energy would be palpable. Instead of going to a nightclub to dance and drink, I would search out gatherings for the purpose of drinking in the divine, getting drunk on the high vibrations of sound, dance and then, silence . . . silence that I could touch, feel and breathe into every pore of my body . . . silence that would connect me to the felt-awareness of my own True Self.

After a while, I slowly shifted into going to Unity church, because it offered what I needed as far as a community for my sons and myself. The Siddha yoga community is so small in Charleston; it was not conducive to including my sons, and the practice of the meditation was too intense for the younger ones. It really is true that we are constantly evolving and changing and that what is perfect for us at one point may shift to something else at another time. While I am not practicing Siddha Yoga or the Yoga with asanas as much these days, it is still very much a part of me, and I know that at some point I may go back to it.

Right now, my main spiritual practice is walking in nature.

It is both my meditation and my physical exercise. It is my yoga. In essence, all that I do right now is a form of yoga. It is a mindful practice of connecting with the Divine Self within and around me. Anywhere from the act of brushing my teeth, being with my children or my husband, preparing a meal or creating art, all have the potential to bring me to the felt-awareness of Source. The process of watching my mind and noticing if it is contracting or expanding, without judgment, is a powerful practice of mindfulness. The more I practice, the more natural and effortless it becomes. I am able to see more clearly when I am moving out of this alignment with Source, and most times, realign more quickly. Life itself has become my spiritual practice. The opportunities for Awakening are endless and are available to us in each present moment. One of those sweet moments came one hot balmy day, right in my front yard, from one of my little gurus.

18

Little Gurus

KAI WAS FOUR YEARS OLD playing basketball with his older brother Chaz in the front yard. All of a sudden, Chaz came rushing in the front door with him in his arms. Kai was bleeding profusely from a cut on his forehead. He had fallen and cut his head open—damn those crocs! I kept thinking I needed to throw those out, as much as he tripped while playing in those plastic, loose-fitting shoes. Thank God Sherman was home, because these kinds of catastrophes are not my strong suit. Sherman took him into the bathroom and surveyed the wound, informing me that we needed to bring him to the emergency room for stitches. I couldn't even look at him; I was so traumatized. But in my hysterical haze, I remembered that the Doctors Care that was just five minutes away recently opened and had weekend hours. I had made a mental note only days before of the hours of operation posted on the sign that we drove by daily. I called, and they said we could bring him right away.

Sherman held our sweet boy in the back seat, keeping his head covered with a compress. He whimpered and cried quietly, as I drove. They brought him to a room immediately to prepare him for stitches. It was a pretty jagged cut since he had fallen on the concrete, and a huge bump was swelling beneath the open gash. As the doctor was dealing with his wound, my baby boy started to chant the Om sound over and over. Sherman was sitting right over him comforting him, and I was sitting over to the side so that I could not see his wound. He was coaching him to breathe and relax, when Kai spontaneously put his hands in prayer position in front of his heart. In his complete state of nonresistance, he chanted what he had heard *me* chant over and over throughout his short life. As a baby, he loved to join me in my yoga practice, and sometimes he would sit in lotus position and Om with me.

I was so amazed by the calm that came over him and the whole room. He was so relaxed that he even had a little grin on his beautiful, blissed-out face. He was able to access this practical and powerful tool to center and calm himself, and yet I could not seem to do it with my twenty or so years of practice. Wow! I was awed and humbled. It was such an amazing moment for me as a mother to realize so poignantly that the greatest gift I can offer my children is to practice my own alignment. It is not what we say that has the strongest influence; it is what we do and what we 'be.' Just by doing my yoga day in and day out, in the middle of the living room, where he could witness and be a part of it, however he chose, was all that was necessary for him to know how to access his inner peace at the most crucial moment. What a triumph! I felt so proud of him. Only once did he yell out, when the doctor put a needle in his head to numb it before stitching. Otherwise, he was so relaxed that Sherman would occasionally have him squeeze his hand to make sure that he wasn't becoming unconscious for fear of a concussion.

Not only was Kai my guru that day, but also Sherman was my hero. I am so grateful for his calm, steady nature in the face of crisis. While I may have been a total wreck throughout that experience, I gained a powerful awareness and felt a deep sense of gratitude and grace fill my heart. I sensed that, while my own spiritual practice had offered my four-year-old son a tool for dealing with this stress, it was *he* that had offered me the most at that moment. These tools are useless unless we use them when it really matters. The mantra is not just meant for those ideal moments of calm meditation, but also in those moments of true-life crisis or when we are in the midst of conditions that are not what we necessarily want. Kai was demonstrating Unconditional Love. In a moment that I myself was unable to do so, he aligned with his true nature, which is Love, and stayed there, regardless of the condition. No story. No resistance. Simply love. Simply him.

Kai continues to be an example of Love and sweet compassion for me. He is always expressing his love for me and others. His heart is tender and open, and now at twelve, he is finding his own way to balance his tender nature with a bit of fierceness. He has been practicing karate for many years now, and I feel this has been a good outlet for him and his sensitive nature. Through karate, he can release some of the intense emotion that can build up in a child as sensitive as he and step into an energy that holds a fierce stance.

His natural tendency towards the practice of Love and harmony, I feel, will be his salvation as he navigates this next tender phase of human development. He has found another passion that allows him to channel his offering of love: the creative preparation of food. The day he realized his true love of cooking, he looked up at me with those huge brown, almond-shaped eyes, lively black curls, and a big smile and said, "I have found my art form, Mom! This must be what it feels like for you to paint."

After twenty years of mothering and thirty years as a spiritual seeker, I now feel equipped to be the guiding light for my sons, in a way that I never have before. I am more committed than ever to practicing Unconditional Love, seeing them in their wholeness, perfection and wellness all the time, even when the facts of their lives may indicate otherwise. Not only do I continue to learn from my sons through their experiences, words and actions, but also I become more and more my own guru as a result of what I have learned through them. I imagine that our lives will be a continuing, expansive process, and our roles as student and teacher will vacillate many times throughout this lifetime, and yet in all experiences, I see myself essentially as the student, forever growing, forever evolving and forever grateful for the gurus in my midst.

19

The Balancer

W E ALL KNOW THE SAYING, "God gives us only what we can handle." I think that is a way to help us feel better when we are struggling through life experiences. It is reassuring to think that somehow we will make it through. I am blessed to have felt a sense of balance in my life. While the contractions have felt intense, and at times long, in relation to the whole picture of my life, there have been fewer moments of contraction than moments of expansion and rest.

The birth of Chaz and all his intensity was a powerful contraction and brought forth powerful desire, and thus, expansion. Noah, however, brought Grace with his arrival four and a half years later. He was the complete opposite of my first warrior-like son. Noah was and is a peacemaker and a balancer of energy. This brought a sense of rest, even though

I was juggling the demands of a newborn, a business, new family dynamics, and postpartum depression.

I remember one day yelling at Chaz in frustration, while Noah, distraught and crying, pleaded with me not to yell at 'Chazzy'. He couldn't have been older than two. I remember nursing Noah and noticing the distinct difference in his energy. He would gently stroke my arm as he nursed, whereas Chaz would claw and cling, often grabbing at my mouth, pulling down my bottom lip. When Chaz was born, it seemed he was wide awake as soon as he came out. He was looking around the room, drinking in everything he saw. I remember thinking about how they say a newborn baby can't see past their mother's face while she is holding them and thinking that was so untrue, like so much of what 'they' tell you. For example, I knew he could see the paintings surrounding him.

However, when I had Noah, he was more like the textbook baby and followed the typical description of the slumbering newborn, asleep more than awake. He seemed content and at peace. Even as a baby, he had a sophisticated sense of humor and seemed to know when to laugh at the right places during a movie that we assumed he was too young to understand. When I was still pregnant with him, I had a reading with a non-physical entity named Joseph, who was being channeled through a woman, not unlike Abraham. She predicted his 'delicious sense of humor' then, and I often think about that now when I witness the nature of my brilliant and very funny son.

My mother said to me, more than once, that she could not have known how different two people could be until she gave birth to me. She was comparing me to my older sister, Sarah. Well, that was definitely my experience with Noah. It was fascinating to observe the stark difference. While the first son was like a rocket at warp speed, wanting to be ahead of wherever he was, this second one was perfectly content to stay right where he was and soak up the view. While Chaz would be playing outside all day, with me pulling him inside to give him water, some food and a ten-minute mandatory break from the intense heat of the sun, Noah would lament that he did not like to go outside to sweat and deal with the bugs. Chaz rode his bike at the age of three, begging us to remove the training wheels. While we had to *insist* that Noah learn to ride a bike when he was seven or eight (or was it ten?), just because we thought it was a skill all people should have. He can ride but rarely does. He just simply was not interested.

Noah loves computers and video games. He loves to make other people laugh, but even more, he just loves to laugh. He would draw and draw and draw these characters inspired by the Pokémon cards and write about each one— what their powers were, their purpose and how they would transform or morph into other versions of themselves. He had a wild imagination and would talk endlessly about a world I could not begin to understand. I would have to stop him, because I would glaze over, as I was overwhelmed by his detail and enthusiasm. I thought he would eventually outgrow this fascination with otherworldly creations and start talking about things that I could follow, but at seventeen, he still goes on these tangents that leave me in the dust. Of course, we are able to find some more down-to-earth things to talk about now as well. I am certain that this quality will be a huge asset in the work that he ends up doing in the future.

I remember wondering, how could one teach one's children compassion? For this was not a strong trait in Chaz. In a moment of insight, I realized that there was only one way, and that was to model it. When Noah was very little, I saw what natural compassion looked like. He was born with it. I feel like he was able to naturally model that for his big brother, who has grown into a very sweet and compassionate being himself.

I am so grateful for the differences between them. It has been, and continues to be, a powerful lesson for me in non-judgment to truly honor the perfection of each one, exactly as they are . . . all three of them. Each one is a unique, complex being with individual needs and desires. Acknowledging that and recognizing their strengths and emphasizing them, has been an important tool in my evolving process as a mother and in the work I do now with the Bach Flowers and Vibrational Healing.

The universe knew that I needed a change of pace and a new perspective, and that is what I got when I was given Noah. For the first time, I felt like I was a good mother. With Chaz, I questioned myself—I floundered and struggled. I probably tried too hard. With Noah, it felt more natural, and I had learned not to be so hard on myself. He balanced the energy in the house. He still does. He is the most balanced person I know. I always marvel at the way he has made it all the way to his junior year in high school without hardly any stress, and he is an exceptional student. He works hard but takes lots of breaks as he goes, pacing himself with funny 'memes' on the internet that make him laugh in between projects and homework and studying. Witnessing this brilliant ability to find balance and to be fully in the moment, therefore enjoying life in this extraordinary and consistent way, has offered me a powerful role model in this beautiful son.

When I began having children, I thought that I wanted a girl, at least one. I certainly did not expect to be the mother of three sons! Each time I was pregnant, I asked for something particular in them: beautiful, robustly healthy and a girl—and specifically with Kai, I asked for the child to be harmonious with our family, *before* requesting it be a girl. I knew in asking for this that I would risk not having a girl, because I was aware that the same gender option could be a better match for the whole dynamic of my family, especially considering that my boys are almost all five years apart in age. Kai fit in so perfectly. I could not have dreamed up a more perfect match. He was in love with his brothers, particularly Noah. They were like two peas in a pod. If they weren't so different in size, you would think they were twins, both visually and in the way they interacted. Noah was the most amazing big brother to Kai . . . unusually so. They got along like an old married couple. They did everything together, and each was content to be with the other—inside, away from the heat and bugs. Although, I think Kai may have been a bit more of an outdoor kid, if his main role model wasn't such a homebody.

I believe that I got exactly what I really wanted when I gave birth to three sons. I thought I wanted something else, based on a story I had in my mind. I came from a family of girls. I have two mothers and three sisters, with only one dad and one brother. We had lots of intense and dynamic women in our family. I really did not understand the male species, and while I was attracted to them as a heterosexual female, I did not have a whole lot of respect for men. I felt that women were superior. I am not sure exactly where I developed this perception, and I wonder if it is from a past lifetime.

Loving and adoring my sons from the inception of their lives, has offered me an opportunity to deconstruct this vague and general sense of superiority that I felt. The intimate connection I have had with these incredible male beings has changed everything. I am now able to see the tenderness, the sensitivity, the intensity, the compassion and the innate connection that they have to Source as equal to that of women. Of course, they also sometimes displayed some negative male stereotypical behavior: self-absorption, poor listening skills, primitive/violent actions. They loved to play-fight with each other. They learned it from their father, the fourth of five brothers. I quickly got used to what felt initially, to me, bizarre and disturbing behavior, which I began to respect as a way for boys to release physical and emotional energy. It *can* be a rather healthy practice, if done with guidelines and respect.

My disposition towards the male gender, prior to my mothering my boys, certainly was not a reflection of my feelings about my father. He was actually very balanced in his male and female energies, being very compassionate and nurturing, and at times, he was even more emotionally maternal than both of my mothers. My position about men, and my ability to appreciate them as a gender, has grown into a deep respect and love, helping me to heal a prejudice that kept me from truly *seeing* this half of the human race. Of course, I made exceptions for the men I knew and loved, but now I have an insight into the nature of the male gender from a more personal and intimate perspective.

So while mothering, in and of itself, has been a powerful facilitator of my awakening, mothering boys, in particular, has been incredibly expanding and has sensitized me to this brilliant and beautiful aspect of humanity that I have come to love and honor, not just as individuals, but as a whole. Wow— that is big! I had not even realized that I would write about this, and as I am, I realize how important and essential this heart-opening, mind-blowing realization is to my personal path in Spiritual Awakening.

We get what we want, what we *really* want, not what

we *think* we want. My Soul knows why I came forth, and so everything that comes to me, that seems like it somehow should not be happening or isn't a part of the plan, could be the very thing that is propelling me into a greater expansion than I could ever imagine.

I thought I wanted daughters, but what I really wanted was to heal my disconnection from half of this glorious human race. I really wanted to see God in every face and to know my Oneness with All that Is. How brilliant this Universe is at delivering exactly what we truly desire!

I consciously planned only one of my pregnancies: Kai—born of human passion and divine grace. My Soul, in its infinite wisdom, designed the perfect blend of characteristics to be present in this son. I feel like my Soul participated with the willing souls of my beautiful sons in a sublime play of consciousness to bring forth the perfect conditions for me to evolve and expand and Awaken. In this intricate web of reality, we all play the perfect role for each other in the way that will best facilitate our desires to evolve.

I wanted these beings, and I wanted them to be boys!
I wanted Chazaray. I wanted Noah. I wanted Kai.
Each is uniquely perfect in his offering.
I am humbled in gratitude for their gift of choosing to come forth as my sons.
I am blessed, so so blessed.

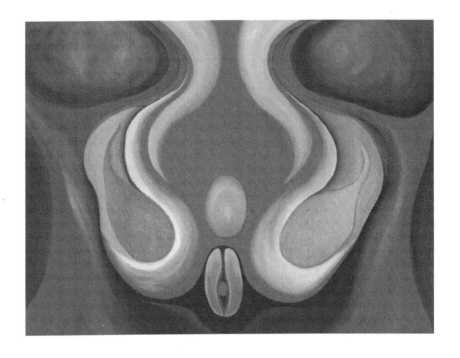

20

Sexuality and God

I N MY EARLY YEARS OF painting, I became aware of a tingling of energy originating in my root chakra, my yoni while I was creating art. Yoni is Sanskrit for womb; sacred space; vagina; the center of creation. I was soon able to make the connection between creative energy and sexual energy, realizing that they were a part of each other. As I contemplated the powerful flow of energy that occurred during the creative process, I felt that this sexual energy was spiritual in nature. This sexual energy can be channeled in many different ways. In our one-dimensional way of looking at sexuality, we have often regulated it to the limited and primitive act of sexual intercourse between two human beings. There has been a sordid history of sex and its place in our society. It has either exalted humanity and the expression of love or has undone humanity with its abuse and divergence from its true form and function.

It is my theory that, when we have learned to express our essential and creative nature, we are able to channel the sexual energy more fluidly. Sexuality was not meant to be confined to the 'bedroom.' Not only is it what makes us human, but it is also a doorway to the Divine. When we are able to allow our sexual energy to flow freely and naturally, it can be expressed in many ways. Our sensual nature is fully realized through the expression and appreciation of art in all its forms. This can be experienced, for example, in the process of creating a beautiful and delectable meal, sharing it with love and consuming it with full awareness, aroused by taste and scent and satiated by the experience and the sustenance. Sexuality is easily seen as expressed through the dancer that taps into the Divine flow, as she powerfully pirouettes on point or sensually undulates movement that is primal and organic. Our sexual nature is unleashed when creating and listening to music that plucks on the inner chords of our heart, opening a dam of passion and connection.

Sexuality connects us to our own Inner Divinity, our most sacred, intimate space, the temple within our bodies that gives us access to our expansive Self, which is unencumbered by the perceived limitations of the human condition. I like to think of our sexuality as the energy of Source embedded within our nature, so that we may feel the impulse to create and express and expand. It is the aspect of humanity that is most divine in its true and fully-realized form, yet it has become one of the most misunderstood and abused aspects of our being human. For many, the concept of God has been archaic and rigid and has come with an exclusive list of what is right and wrong. The same is true for our concept of sexuality and the role it plays in our lives. Of course, many of the distorted perceptions of sexuality originated from the very institutions that profess expertise in the nature of God.

I feel that, if our children are encouraged to find and express their passions creatively, the pubescent urges that arise as they become more aware of their sexual nature, will have healthy channels of expression, and they may not feel the compulsion to have sexual intercourse as early in life. They must have an outlet for this powerful energy surge, or its potential to be explosive later or sooner in their life is high. The most detrimental approach to burgeoning sexuality is to try to keep it under lock and key. The act of sex is only one way in which our sexuality is felt and expressed. When it is seen in its wholeness, as a flow of creative energy that yearns to be released and shared, and it *can be* in so many ways, then we are not limited to sex as the only means to express this human and divine energy.

I dream of a time when we celebrate the sexuality of our young ones and allow their natural river to flow without hindrance; a time when we simply step out of the way and allow what is natural to occur, no shaming, embarrassing, controlling or warning them; a time when we honor the sensuality of our humanity in all its aspects and let our children know, when they dance and sing and eat and share love, love of all kinds, that this sexual energy is a natural part of it all, and we do not need to be afraid of it; a time when we do not teach our children that our sexual nature should be contained and confined behind locked doors. This very approach is what cultivates deviant and distorted sexual behavior. Freedom of what is natural cultivates healthy, loving, mindful, compassionate, conscious, sensitive adults, not the suppression of it.

One of the most delicious parts of our sexuality is indeed

expressed through sexual exchange with another human being and is a profound opportunity for sharing love and Oneness with another. Sexuality is also a sensation and awareness that can be felt within yourself, and the expression of it can be as diverse as the humans expressing it, through self-love, art or in the mind and heart of one practicing mindfulness, being fully aware of the sensual experience of each divine moment. Our human senses give us the most Divine experiences. It is our physicality that both divorces us from our Divinity, and yet contains the perfect ingredients for reunification with our Divine nature. One of those ingredients is our sexual nature, which is intrinsically one with our ability to feel and experience through our five senses. Such a brilliant design!

When we suppress this innate need to create and express through our sexual nature, what was initially meant as a key to divinity, becomes a tool for destruction, hatred, self-gratification, domination, possessiveness, jealousy, control and so on.

It is our disconnection with the Divine and its true purpose that allows for us to behave in any way that denies Divinity in ourselves or another. Ironically, the pious and puritan values of many religious institutions have bred behaviors in their followers that are sexually deviant. I believe this is a result of the suppression—the cutting off of the flow of what is not only natural but that which is Divine Energy Itself!

Wow! I know that is an intense and passionate statement. I contemplated and journaled about this concept years ago. This idea of the creative and sexual energy as one is very much a part of the wordless, yet bold expression of my art that is conveyed and felt through the heart and the senses, not the mind.

While I love lively and engaging discussion, I am not much

for debates, and I am certainly not one to proselytize. It is my desire only to share my inspired thoughts that feel like resonance and passion within me. I am only an expert in my own divine connection to Source, my own personal path to Awakening. I love that my way is not the only way and that the diversity amongst us is as deep as it is vast. I love that I only have to know what I know and what I am inspired to know and that that is enough. So, with that said, I offer my view with respect and love for all the paths to God and inner truth, with the awareness that some paths take us on winding and perilous terrain that, at times, seems the antithesis of Divine Love. Certainly, the way in which humanity has dealt with the issue of sexuality has been complex and manifold. What to me seems like the most obvious basis for sexuality in humans, for the experience and expression of love, passion, creative energy and the conception of new life, has become incarcerated by disconnected minds trying to control something that is uncontrollable . . . God.

God is Love. God cannot be contained, and when we try to control the flow of Divine Love, Divine Chaos becomes human chaos. As we all know, *that* is not a pretty sight. However, in the grand scheme, All Is Well, and nothing is ever truly lost. All paths contain contractions for this propulsion forward, and all paths lead us back to the heart and consciousness of God . . . eventually.

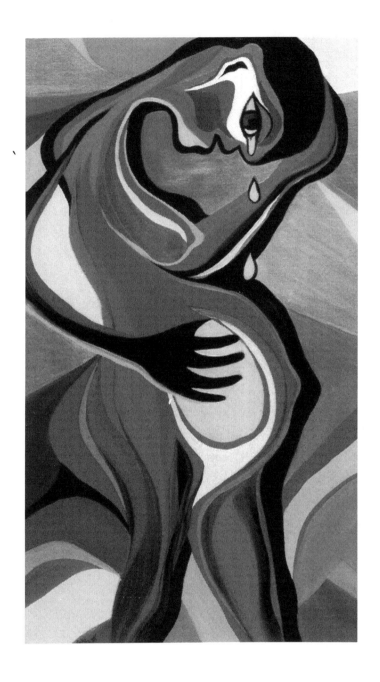

21

Money, Safety and Loss

WHEN NOAH WAS THREE, AND Chaz was eight, I got pregnant. It was unexpected, somewhat like the first two. This time, however, we did not take it in stride. Sherman freaked out, and then, I did too. For a whole week, we contemplated whether we could mentally or emotionally handle another child. To be honest, I remember my first response to the positive test result was excitement, then I became pensive. And when Sherman's reaction was to contract, it triggered fear in me as well.

There was a lot going on in our lives at the time. It was a tough period. My husband was coming to terms with dissolving the business, NuSouth, that he had put so much energy into, and that we both felt so sure would be wildly successful. While it *was* successful in raising consciousness around the critical issue of racism in America and became of symbol of healing, and social change, financially it became unsustainable.

Self-esteem and self-worth were precarious for us both, and for the first time that I can remember, we were feeling cut off from the eternal flow of Source Energy . . . in the form of money.

Money had always come easily to me. No one would call me rich, but my personal relationship with the flow of prosperity was gentle and fluid, and I always had enough. At a young age, I had decided that I would not work more than twenty-four hours a week. I was an artist, and I needed to have time to create my art. This was a priority for me. I recognized by the time I was working, at the age of eighteen, that painting was essential to my spiritual and emotional well-being. It kept me balanced, because it was my way of plugging into my Source, my Divine Self.

I look back at that declaration now and see how powerful that stance was—my point of attraction, steered by my vibrational offering, set the tone for my relationship to money, work and time. Even with my own business, at the tender age of nineteen, I only worked three days a week, for the most part. In our current business, Utopia, I am only scheduled to be in the shop three days a week as well. It has always been this way. I have created a life rich in time to create and explore my spiritual development, as well as time to be with my sons. Sherman and I both have been able to do this, and this is the kind of wealth I value most.

I believe that during this time of contraction, neither of us were feeling worthy of the flow of money, because we were feeling guilty and responsible for the loss of money that family and friends had invested in the business that we had such high hopes for. I share this now, aware of the feeling of tension that arises when I speak of it, but I am also aware of the importance of the story of money in our lives and how valuable it is to face our patterns of thought and stories that we have about money. I believe that money is energy, like everything else, and that it responds to our vibrational offering, like everything else. Prior to this, I always felt comfortable with the flow of money. I felt deserving of it. I felt confident in my ability to make it, or now I would say, attract it.

During this period, I became aware that the reason for the decrease in the flow was directly connected with the feeling of not deserving it. It had been completely unconscious, and therefore, incredibly difficult. When this realization arose within me years later, I immediately felt the relief and was able to begin to recover from this self-inflicted poverty consciousness. Our business Utopia experienced the contraction of this energy flow, and we struggled to keep afloat. It was an incredibly powerful lesson in so many ways and particularly around self-worth and money and the law of attraction.

The news of this pregnancy fell on the heels of these struggles. Sherman's stress and disappointment were palpable, but he did not have a healthy outlet to truly process it, so it remained a latent energy, unresolved within him, and to some degree, in me as well. After a week of considering our options, I remember my beautiful, sweet husband taking my hand and pulling me onto the couch next to him. Looking into my eyes with love, he said that we were going to have this baby, that we had too much love not to share it with this new life. He assured me, and himself, that everything would be fine. We embraced, and I wept with relief.

I marveled at the ease I felt with this pregnancy, not experiencing any of the expected nausea that I endured in the first trimester with the others. Of course, I dreamt of having a girl and became excited at this prospect. When one finds out one is going to have a baby, a whole life is born in the mind of the parents. A future is conceived and imagined in the mind, while the new life grows in the mother's womb. It is all a story. Nothing is real until it is actually happening. Then, it comes to pass, and the reality evolves into something else. Each moment is new and full of potential.

One hot night in August during my first trimester, the two boys and I were home in our beds. Sherman was out at a boxing party, and I had just turned the light out to go to sleep. It must have been midnight when I heard the sounds of footsteps outside my bedroom door dragging down the hallway. It did not sound like Sherman, and I hadn't heard the front door open. I called out his name anyway. My heart was pounding in my chest. No answer. I heard some other noises and then nothing. I was shaking as I picked up the phone to call my neighbor. I wanted someone who was close and did not even think of calling the police. I was terrified. The neighbor came over with phone in hand and the police on the other line. When he arrived at the front door, I ventured out of my room to discover the back door open. The amateur intruder had made his escape out the back and out the side gate of my backyard. Since we only had one car and Sherman was out, he must have thought the house was empty.

It was so traumatizing that my sense of safety had been shaken, and I felt completely vulnerable. The time following the break-in, which was another manifestation of the insecurity that we were feeling in relationship to money, became a time of exploring the concept and spiritual nature of 'safety'. Just like the time when I wanted to cultivate untouchable, unconditional JOY, I gave birth to another powerful desire— to know and experience the feeling of SAFETY, regardless of the conditions in my life. This was a huge contraction that was bringing forth massive yearning for relief. This literal manifestation of vulnerability, of feeling violated from some force outside myself, was truly a reflection of my point of attraction. I was creating my reality by thinking thoughts of loss and disappointment. I felt that these negative circumstances were out of my control, and at the same time, I felt responsible for them, and Sherman, I believe, felt the same. Sherman and I were both in the state of mind that was a match to the break-in. Of course, at the time, I could not see that. I was sinking in the quicksand of insecurity.

It was not too long after this incident that I had a miscarriage. Devastated by the loss of the imagined future of the daughter I never had, we planted a tree and rose bush for the memory of a dream . . . a child that was not meant to be. This baby may not have been the one to come into our lives in the way we imagined, but she was the catalyst that gave birth to desire. She opened the door to my heart, offering me the gift of yearning, yearning for a child. This was a sensation I had never experienced before. All the other pregnancies were unplanned. While they were still conceived from love, they were not consciously chosen prior to conception. Chosen, yes, *after* conception, but not before.

The lost baby became the one to open my heart to the son who did eventually come through. I grew consumed with the desire to have another child. We decided to wait a while to get clear about what we really wanted. I knew what I wanted. Sherman needed time. I marinated in the sensation of yearning, desire and brooding for a baby. It was a new feeling, and it felt good. I was in no big hurry. I waited for the perfect time to reveal itself. As the Universe always works in its mysterious and synchronistic ways, the perfect time arose from yet another powerful and intense contraction!

22

Opening

AMAZINGLY, LIFE GOES ON AFTER a miscarriage, a home invasion and even after 9/11. A week or two after the miscarriage, the ultimate manifestation embodying the lack of safety that I was feeling, came in the form of the twin towers in New York City being hit by two planes on September 11, 2001. The whole country became a macrocosmic reflection of my, and perhaps many people's, microcosmic fear. I think that most of us on this planet have been living a conditional life—a life that requires certain conditions to feel safe and aligned with Love. We don't know any better. We don't realize that we have a choice, and that with the practice of mindfulness and awareness, we are the creators of our own reality, and we can begin to find our way out of this painful trap of helplessness and of being a victim of fate or chance. While we may not be able to control all external conditions, we may begin to take ownership of our feelings, our thoughts and our vibrational stance and begin to affect conditions in our own experience, which will ultimately create change through a ripple effect that reaches many. The practice of Alignment and Unconditional Love has the profound potential to free us from debilitating fear—at least that has been my experience.

For a while, the feeling of vulnerably within me escalated, and this was mirrored by a nation reeling from the shock and terror of this unprecedented attack on American soil. While this country is no stranger to war, it has not experienced war on its own soil for generations. I was in shock from the break-in and lived with a nagging fear that it would happen again, feeling unsafe within my own home. I was also in shock that my own body had betrayed me, dispelling this dream of a future, a child, a daughter.

Within this climate of insecurity, an intense and long contraction ensued, and yet all contractions ultimately propel us forward, bringing forth a new life, a new perspective and an evolved Self. Something had to give. It all came to a head when my relationship seemed to be in jeopardy. A series of events and misunderstandings led to a huge, horrible, heated argument between us. I could not believe what was happening, and yet in retrospect, it was understandable that an explosion like this would occur after the buildup of unresolved tension that stemmed from a parallel erosion of security within our psyches. Sherman and I rarely argued at this point in our marriage. We had been through a lot together, and yes, we would have the occasional disagreement and stressful exchange, but nothing like this. My fear and neediness for him to understand and resolve this issue were so intense and heart-wrenching that not until he threw a glass bowl across the room, did I wake up out of my pitiful haze of insanity. Shocking himself with his own fury, he left the house and subsequently found a therapist, straight out of the phone book the very next day. He felt he needed help to sort through some of the confusion and intense emotions that he was experiencing.

The result of this powerful and explosive release gave birth to a period of expansion and passion and awakening in our relationship. For Sherman, it was a huge awakening and a release of so much pent-up emotional torment from the feelings of self-blame, disappointment and lost dreams relating to his business, not to mention the feelings of helplessness to protect our children and me, after the break-in and the miscarriage. I was not fully aware of the amount of stress he was carrying; I was so consumed with my *own* devastation from the loss and feelings of insecurity. In retrospect, we were ripe for transformation. The sand in the oyster was polishing the pearl of our passion for each other, our family and the beautiful life we already had. Until this argument, we could not seem to see or feel this passion, as we were blinded by our identification with the illusion of disconnection and loss.

The weeks and months that followed this re-awakening of our love for each other and ourselves, was a time of beautiful and passionate expression. It was like we had just fallen in love all over again. We made love every moment we could. We could not keep our hands off each other. It was intense, sexy and heart opening. I felt alive and connected again to this man I had adored for so long, and we were able to drown out all the pain that brought us to this place of passion, lust and longing. It was delicious and illuminating and liberating. It was a time of such intense passion that I worried there would be a devastating deflation once the momentum of our expansion, the propulsion of life force that proceeded the long, painful contraction we had both endured, lost its impetus. I know now that my worry was a reflection of my underdeveloped sense of inner security. Understandably, I was still grappling with the issue of safety and wondered if this newfound passion would fizzle, leaving me high and dry and emotionally deflated. Now I know better than to engage in such limiting and self-sabotaging thoughts. I care too much about how I feel to allow such a train of thought to get momentum. Of course, that does not mean that my thoughts don't occasionally get the best of me. However, my commitment to my sanity, to my freedom and to the practice of mindfulness and Unconditional Love keeps me vigilant. I watch my thoughts and then I notice whether that thought makes me feel good or bad. If the thoughts make me feel good, I know I am in alignment with my Source and with my own desires.

I was not as vigilant then, although I had begun the process of Awakening and was definitely practicing some mindfulness even then. In spite of this feeling of an impending shift from this captivating reunion of deep and searing passion with my husband, I was enjoying the wave of ecstasy that enraptured me with his new-found release and Awakening. It was a sweet and inspiring time, and with the blend of lust, love and a deep yearning for the baby we had lost, we eagerly opened our hearts to the idea and reality of conceiving our next child.

Kai was born out of a powerful momentum of energy. We blissfully embraced this conscious choice to bring forth life from love. It was such a divinely beautiful process to choose this conception, and *he* was equally as divinely beautiful. When he came forth, his predominate quality of being was one of Love. I always described him as emotionally intelligent, even as a very young child. As a baby, he could sense the energy of those in a room and would gravitate to those who needed extra love and reassurance. It was like a sixth sense that made him know where his love was most needed. He is a lover. He was certainly born of pure and conscious connection to love. What a blessing! Such powerful contractions brought forth such a beautiful manifestation of love in the form of my beautiful, sweet son. I had been carrying this story that I wanted a daughter, and yet that story paled in comparison to the gift I received when the Universe sent me Kai

Life could not be more kind. Reality could not be more perfect. When I look at the whole picture of all that ebbing and flowing, contracting and expanding, faltering and flying, fearing and freedom I am amazed and humbled by the perfection and beauty of this magnificent tapestry we call Life. How could it be more perfect—to lose the dream for a beautiful reality—a reality that rivals any imagined story I could have ever dreamed? From the perspective I now hold in this very moment, after telling the uncomfortable story of contraction so that I could share the expansion and relive that too, taking me beyond the story into the reality of life, I am humbled by the way the Divine plan unfolded. I am inspired to trust Life, to let it freely unravel. I have chosen this grand adventure with the whole of me, the deepest part of me, the most expansive part of me. I am inspired to remember that it is all good in the grand scheme of things, and that even when I am feeling discomfort, fear or pain, mild or excruciating, all is well, all is a part of the process, and Life is being born from this contraction. All contractions are productive. All contractions give birth to Life—breathtaking, transformative, extraordinary, awe-inspiring LIFE. I choose to ride the wave and find the thrill in the up and the down of it, to remember the joy in pain and the love in loss. I choose to open my heart and risk vulnerability for authentic connection. I choose to accept myself in all stages of my Awakening.

23

Peace and Passion

*"Passion without Peace
is flight
endless flight
without a place to land
when the wings are weary."*

F OR MY FORTIETH BIRTHDAY, SHERMAN gave me the best gift ever. He designed and self-published a book of my art. I had been saying I needed to do this for years. I had many of my paintings already photographed. He managed to do it without me knowing. I was shocked and moved and very grateful. Sherman anticipated that I might want to go back into the program and edit the book, and I was grateful he did. I added poetry and paintings, and yet the original was beautiful and complete unto itself. The title of the book is *Peace and Passion*. I feel like those two words truly encompass the essence of my art, as well as my personal approach to life.

Peace and Passion

I am passionate about Peace.
It is the essence of what I desire more than anything else . . .
the sensation of peace

Peace is a passionate place
that resides deep
in the red hot crevices
of my heart

It is soothing
and sensuous
It is sexy and expansive
It is ecstasy
and the deep sleep
that follows a passionate
release.

It is the place
felt
after resistance
yields
to surrender.

It is commitment
to the innermost
intimate place
that when we touch it
we open to
the most ecstatic
passionate

FREEDOM

Passion without Peace
is an amputation
a limb without the body to
ground it
into the lush
delicious
silence

Passion without Peace
is flight
endless flight
without a place to land
when the wings are weary.

Passion is Peace
the expression of all that Peace knows
They are the yin and the yang of each other

I choose Peace
first
and then may the wings of Passion
carry me
into the unknown realms
that Peace would have me know

Then . . .
may Passion
open me
render me helpless
to control its joy
its vast, endless, bottomless pit
of Love . . . expressed

May Peace surrender me to Passion
and may Passion
open my heart
fearlessly to
All that Is

All.
That.
Is!

24

An Invitation

L IFE OFFERS US MANY INVITATIONS for growth and expansion, opportunities to practice the revelations we receive along the way. I believe that, if we can begin to reframe the experiences that arise in our lives, the ones that cause us pain, torment, irritation, discomfort, impatience, etc., then we can develop less resistance within us and transform the experience into a compelling opportunity for growth. Remember my story of yoga and how we were guided to redefine our perception of 'pain' to that of 'sensation' at varying degrees of intensity? Just that simple shift in awareness, practicing a new definition, a new word to describe a physical sensation, can be incredibly powerful and can alter the trajectory of our lives in more profound ways than we can imagine.

I am more aware of the way in which I approach my body when it is out of balance. I am conscious of my reactions, my words and my resistance to what is happening. I am aware that the sensation we call pain can be intense and uncomfortable, but that suffering is optional. The suffering arises from our minds, from our resistance to the sensation we describe as pain. The story that we attach to the sensation is the true suffering: "I am dying. Maybe I am having an aneurysm. I must have breast cancer, since it runs in the family. What if it is shingles? I know people who have said that it was the worst pain they ever experienced." It can go on and on, but the sensation is simply that—a sensation. The *story* about the sensation is the real torture.

The mind is a very dangerous thing when we allow it to run rampant. Most of us don't realize that we have a choice about suffering or about what thoughts arise in us that cause it. Most of us think we are suffering because our body is experiencing a physical condition that is out of our control and that it is normal for us to be upset about it. We even feel it would be irresponsible for us not to delve into the possible cause and treatments, which often cause us more stress, fear, confusion and physical pain. Then when we feel that 'pain', our negative thinking expands and grows until the suffering is unbearable. At that breaking point, there is usually a breakthrough, and instead of negative thoughts expanding, there is an expansion of consciousness, a surrender to the Divine, and when surrender *does* occur, relief follows. With relief comes an expansion. It may be describable, palpable . . . or it may be elusive and vague but visceral all the same. The birthing process goes on . . . contracting, opening, contracting, expanding.

Mindfulness is a moment-by-moment practice. It is about watching the thinking that arises and not believing all of our thoughts. It is about soothing ourselves back into alignment when we slip into unconsciousness. It is soft and gentle and easy. Practicing mindfulness as much as possible is a commitment to ourselves and our own well-being. It is about refocusing our attention to bring us back into alignment when we start to feel negative emotion.

I love this practice and realize that the invitations for expansion continue to come but with less resistance. By cultivating mindfulness and Unconditional Love, the sensation of discomfort has lessened, and a feeling of excitement and gratitude for the opportunity has taken its place. It is a delicious thing to be open to the feelings that arise, even when they are feelings of resistance. Underneath the discomfort, there is a knowing that all is well and that this too has a purpose . . . like a mother's contractions during birth.

One day, not long after my new understanding of the concept of Unconditional Love, I was on my way to the park for my morning walk. I was following behind a truck with a trailer attached to it. He was pulling into his parking spot, and as I proceeded to drive behind him, he began to back up. I laid in on my horn twice, attempting to warn him that I was behind him. He was furious with me. He flipped me 'the finger', which I was able to witness from his side mirror. I looked at him somewhat apologetically, mouthing that I did not know he was going to back up. Of course, he could not hear me. I felt startled and surprised by his reaction, but continued to park my car. He hit his horn and began to back up like he wanted to scare me. I felt confused by his hostility. It is very rare that I am confronted with such intense negative energy. I parked and got out of my car to see him pulling up behind me. He rolled down his window to yell at me. I told him I did not know he was going to back up, and he screamed that I did not have to act that way. Apparently, he perceived *me* as being hostile towards *him*, or at the very least, he saw me as being inappropriate. He went to park after this disturbing exchange, and I decided it would not be wise for me to leave my car there in the same area as him, so I found another place to park.

Frazzled and confused by this intense and aggressive interaction, I began my walk through the wooded path of my beautiful park that always has a way of bringing me back into alignment. At first, I was full of unaligned thoughts. I considered the possibilities that made this man so hostile. I thought things like, "Angry white racist! Will he come get me and hurt me? He was crazy and ignorant. What an asshole! Will I be safe in my park anymore? I hope I don't bump into him on my walks. Why was he so upset? I was right. *He* was in the wrong." Blah, blah, blah, blah. . . .

Then I remembered, maybe half a mile into my walk, "Unconditional Love . . . Deep breath . . . Awareness. When I think this thought, do I feel aligned with Love? No. No. No. Do I need to love this stranger to feel Love? No. Love requires no condition to be present. It is what I am. I am love. I am using the thoughts of this man to keep me from the awareness of the Love that I am. I do not need to love him. I need to *be* the love that I am. Unconditional Love. Breathe. Relief. Sweet, subtle relief. Alignment. I am safe. I am connected to Divine wisdom. I have been invited to practice Unconditional Love." Tingles and goosebumps began to reflect my growing connection. I began to feel joy arise within me—unconditional joy rippled through me, opening my heart.

New thoughts began to surface about this stranger, "He is Love too. Maybe I startled him, and the fear he felt when he heard my horn made him reactive and out of control. Perhaps he feels bad for behaving so reactively."

That story felt less uncomfortable. I could feel Love when I reached for thoughts that were more compassionate. I did not have to reach too far once I felt the alignment—a result of my commitment to Love without condition. When I noticed I was feeling like shit, I realized I was not *in* Love. I was being conditional about my alignment.

By the end of my walk, I was practically floating, exhilarated by this process, by this reawakening to the Love that I am, that he is, that All is. I was full of gratitude for this opportunity to practice myself back into Love. I was grateful that it was a stranger and not my son or husband that facilitated, through contrast, this blessed opportunity for expansion. Each time we realign with our True Self, we are more than we were before. Our new awareness is accumulating energy and offering more and more to the whole of Us. It is an Expanding Universe, and we are propelling this expansion. We are that important—each one of us. The rhythmic flow of life is a process of contracting and expanding, ebbing and flowing, opening and closing. This is the rhythm of life that we all yearn to experience. We desire variety, diversity. We desire the dance as well as the rest, the sitting. We desire the sweet and the savory, the joy and the sorrow, the fear and the love. It all offers the awareness of the other and the knowledge of what we now want. These emotions are the texture of human life. The contractions invite us into life, to our own unfolding.

As each invitation from life arises in the form of something that is seemingly unwanted, remember what I now remember: Breathe deeply and do not resist. Allow the rhythm of your Awakening to take you on the ride of your life. Open your heart, let the Divine Pulse take over, and you will be delivered to the light and love that is your birthright.

25

CONTRACTION and the Pain Body

NOT MORE THAN A COUPLE of days after writing about the story of the man in the park yelling at me and expressing my gratitude for the opportunity to practice Unconditional Love, I was offered another invitation for expansion. It was Easter day. I was feeling a bit out of alignment for moments throughout the day. There was no real reason for it. It was the full moon, and my cycle was a week or less away. I may have been a bit more fragile than usual. I hosted a gathering of family and a few new friends. It was all going well, although I did notice that my OCD (Obsessive Compulsive Disorder) tendencies had heightened over the last couple days, especially with regards to the house. I really wanted it to be orderly and beautiful.

When I saw Sherman walking with the phone outstretched toward me, I was in the middle of eating dessert and talking with the guests. I motioned that I didn't want to talk and would call whoever it was back. He practically growled at me, and with a frown, he pushed the phone into my hand. He scornfully told me to take the phone and to talk to my sister. I was shocked and hurt and humiliated. He never speaks to me like that! And he did it in front of other people. It was painful. I felt a contraction beginning, and any teetering that I was feeling before became a full-blown wobble right out of alignment with my Divine Self. I became unplugged, derailed and completely identified with the ego. As I was on the phone, he started washing dishes. I walked by him, and he threw me another look of disgust. I flipped him the finger, just like the man in the park did to me! His energy felt so hostile I wanted to run out of the house and get as far away from him as possible, but I had company. I pulled him away from the dishes, back to our room, to confront him with what I felt had just happened. He felt in the right and felt that I was wrong and hostile towards him. I was shocked. It is amazing how two people can see things so differently yet be experiencing the same thing. The very feeling I felt was coming *from* him, created the reality I then experienced *with* him. It was a vibrational match. I was feeling pulled into the familiar human approach to relationship and to love, in other words, conditional. I was feeling out of Love with myself, disconnected, deflated and disappointed with him. I was even more disappointed with myself for not being able to find the Unconditional Love in me for me. At that moment, I certainly could not find it for him. But what I know is, when I am Unconditionally Loving, then I am not resisting any conditions that arise. I am not derailed by the condition, so I am able to stay connected not only to the Love that *I am*, but also to the Love that *he is*. I do not let the condition of his unwanted behavior become bigger than the Love that I have for him or for myself.

As I write, I am feeling some relief. I am writing as a way

to re-align, to practice the awareness of Unconditional love. I notice that it is best that I don't focus on him and the condition that triggered me to disconnect, because it brings me back to the feeling of pain and hurt, sadness and anger. That is a lot of disconnected thinking. It is a very slippery slope down the rabbit hole. Of course, going to sleep and starting over tomorrow would be helpful, yet it feels more important to shift out of the pattern of thought that is causing the pain. I want to clear the energy within me, so I won't pick it back up when I wake. I want to soothe my way back to the place where I align with the Love that I am, regardless of anything or anyone in my midst. I don't need him to be nice or happy, polite or understanding for me to feel good. If I do, then I am not free—I am trapped in a conditional life that leaves my happiness at the hands of others. I desire to be happy now *and* when I wake up. I am holding my attention on the things that make me feel good and not on the conditions that caused the disconnection with mySelf, with Source and with my partner.

After shifting my perspective, I was able to dose off to sleep. Throughout the night, I had a dream that was disturbing. I felt sensations in my body that were very uncomfortable. I felt periods of ease and rest, then more periods of discomfort. Sherman came to bed after I fell asleep, and his presence in the bed was okay with me. The resistance I had felt toward him, and the story I had made up about him, was finally subsiding, but the feeling of unease in my body continued. My 'pain body', as described by Eckhart Tolle, had been triggered, and I was identifying with the memory stored in my body that resembled the condition that triggered my disconnection with Source the night before. It is amazing how the emotional body not only responds to traumatic moments through negative emotion, but also how it immediately affects the body through physical discomfort. It is no wonder that people walk around this planet with terrible diseases and ailments in the body. I could feel the resistance within me quickly becoming a physical sensation.

While the anger was no longer dominating my thinking and my energy field, I was feeling the toxicity of it within me and feeling a need to detox. When I saw Sherman in the morning, I easily spoke to him without the feeling of resentment and disdain. Only hours before, I thought I would never be able to release these negative emotions. I knew I would have the opportunity to process this 'contraction' that I was still moving through with my friends, whom I meet with every Monday morning for the purpose of Awakening through conscious awareness. Together we support one another on this journey. Usually, it is six of us, but on this particular Monday, it was only three of us, and we met at my house instead of my mother's. Since we were a small group, I indulged them in my process by reading to them the previous chapter about the man in the park and explained to them what had happened with Sherman. Just reading my own words was powerful for me. How serendipitous this incident with Sherman was. I had just written the story of this man, and I myself reflected his behavior in my reaction to Sherman's perceived assault with flipping him the finger, just as this man did to me in reaction to my blowing the horn at him. I had even felt gratitude that this lesson of Unconditional Love was offered through the contrasting experience with a stranger instead of with my husband or son. Less than a week later, I was given the opportunity to practice Unconditional Love in the face of a more intimate, and therefore, more challenging scenario. This is why I say it is easier to be unconditional with a stranger than it is with those we love most. My requirements for alignment with my husband and sons have more conditions for me to stay aligned with Love, Joy and Freedom. I care too much about the condition, which keeps me from the intimacy of the moment and from the one I love. We think of 'caring' as a good thing, a noble thing, a natural and loving response to another person. Yet, if I look more closely, caring can become a form of resistance to something that is present. If I care that you are sick or in pain or dying, then I can become consumed by feelings that take me away from being fully present with what is and with the person experiencing the conditions. If I am in pain from my caring, I can't be there for you when you are in pain. If I care what these visitors think of Sherman and me and our relationship, then I am identified with the ego and disconnected from the truth of who I am and who Sherman is . . . who he *truly* is. If I care that my son is healthy, drug-free and happy, then I require these conditions to be present for me to feel happy, healthy and even drug-free . . . from the drugs that ease my headaches and other physical conditions that may arise from the pain of this caring and conditional living. When I don't care, I am free, and then I am free to be intimate with what is, intimate with the son whether he is high or sober and intimate with the husband whether he is grumpy or affectionate. I am free from the pain that is created in me when I resist what is. I am free from the story of how things should be, so that I can be present with what is.

To not care is as radical a concept as that of Unconditional Love. My understanding of these concepts is not the traditional understanding. It is interesting to think about how the general public believes it is acceptable and even expected to care by feeling bad or to love only under certain conditions, yet still calling it unconditional.

In some cases, the term unconditional love is understood to mean allowing 'bad' behavior and disregarding one's own alignment in the process—a very misguided viewpoint. We are told to love them when they are beating us, to love them when they are raping us, lying to us, breaking our hearts. This is not Unconditional Love; this is an impossible moral standard that makes us feel bad about ourselves for not being able to live up to it. I thought I loved my sons unconditionally, because I cared so much about them, and because the feeling of intense emotion and caring can feel like love. Sometimes caring can feel good. Sometimes I swell with joy, admiration and gratitude just being in their lovely presence. In those cases, I am either feeling alignment from within, or they are behaving in ways that are inspiring the positive emotion.

Of course, when they are behaving 'badly', in a way that is hurtful I don't feel good, and for that time of disconnection, I am going against my true nature, and I experience pain and suffering. Our thoughts about the person we 'love' are no longer loving. When 'bad' things are happening, and we struggle and resist, we do not have access to the Infinite Intelligence of the Universe that offers solutions and creative ways to bring forth the desired experience and manifestation. We become unplugged from this flow. Of course, sometimes, when we commit to our alignment with Love, we are inspired to remove ourselves from certain conditions, especially when they pose a real threat to our well-being. Other times the conditions transform in the presence of Love that is Unconditional.

I have begun to see Love as a state of being and not so much an action. I *am* Love, rather than I am loving. When I am in that awareness of that which I am, I experience the alignment that produces emotions of joy, passion, freedom, peace and so on. When I am solidly aligned with Love, everything that I encounter from this state is a brilliant reflection of Divine Love. Love is so much more free than being caring. Love sees the perfection of all that is and is not running away from anything. Even though we may perceive something as beautiful or ugly, love allows it all without judgement and sees it all through the eyes of Itself. Love is God. When you care, you have a preference for how things should be. Love doesn't care. Love is complete unto Itself. Love knows all is well, that we are all Love, loved and lovable. It is unconditional. It is inclusive. "It is content with the low places that people disdain." (Byron Katie)

Love resists nothing.

My brilliant, wise and aware comrades sat as my doulas, supporting me with the words that reinforced my deeper knowing, coaxing me to my remembering, bearing witness to my birthing and offering comfort through the contractions. Bradley offered the thought that, as we become more aware when incidents arise, we are more sensitive to the feeling of being out of alignment. We are not as comfortable with the feeling that is less than joy, less than love, peace and ease. We cannot tolerate the feelings that for some may be a way of life. At the beginning of this book, I described the time in my life when I was so accustomed to a constant hum of stress that I did not even know it. Only when I would get a blessed break from it, and the humming buzz stopped, did I realize how good I could feel.

Now, I feel good most of the time. I love life and the life I am creating. What was so shocking to me about the exchange with Sherman is that we were having such a negative interaction. I said to him: "We don't do this!" I couldn't believe it was happening. I was blaming him, but now I see that I was as much a part of perpetuating that nastiness. He even said with an angry tone, "You are mirroring me!" He was right, but I wasn't ready in that red-hot moment to admit it. Ha! As I write that, I actually feel a bit of a smile within me. I now get the humor that was in the drama all along. Wow!

Twelve hours before the discussion with my friends, I had completely identified with the ego, and now I see the whole thing from a more aligned perspective, one where I can feel joy and love regardless of the incident. I am no longer identified with the story. I am no longer attached to the story that would have me wracked in pain, sadness and hurt, a story that would keep me from a home with harmony, joy and laughter. I know better than believe the story of my husband, born of my ego. And because I know better, I had hoped that I would pop out of this addictive, egoic thought process and move back into alignment more quickly and with less pain. Those thoughts made me angry and disappointed, not only with him, but also with myself.

So, I offer a new piece of the puzzle as a result of this Awakening. Be gentle with yourself. Allow for the contractions to come and go without judging the length of time it takes to move through the labor. Let the birth have its life and its timing. Try not to add resistance to resistance. Once the momentum begins to build, there is no stopping the process of expansion. Try to remain as Awake as possible and know that the labor will eventually come to an end.

I feel grateful, grateful for this process, for this opportunity to share this story as it happened. I feel grateful for the release and relief I am now experiencing, grateful for all the players in my drama, especially Sherman, knowing that our souls are blissfully enjoying the dance of our becoming!

26

OPEN HEART

A N OPEN HEART DOES NOT ache. Like an open mind, it is unconditional. It is open to all that shows up, like a flower in full bloom, it does not require anyone to witness its beauty or its openness. It is natural for the heart to open, when it is time. When the mind is open, it allows the heart to open. When the mind is open, it is empty of concepts that keep it from experiencing the open heart. The open heart does not protect itself from perceived danger, because it is beyond thought, and the 'other' does not exist in this open space. Only the One is real in the open mind and the open heart. There is no I or you. There is only Love, and the open heart is being, experiencing and expressing this Love.

The open heart feels joyous and free. The aching and the pain are experienced when the heart is contracting, constricting its natural state of openness. The heart contracts when the mind closes and identifies with stories about hurt, pain, rejection, abandonment, self-sacrifice, resentment. . . It contracts when the mind believes the story that something should be different from what is. An open heart is evidence of an Awakened mind.

The open heart gives freely, without expectation or exception. It gives so that it may feel and be. The open heart receives without need, riding the waves of its own fulfillment. The open heart opens to receive the light and air that sustains it and gives by its very opening.

When you feel the opening of your heart, your blossoming is at hand, and your Awakening will reveal the Divine You to you. Divine Love will render you helpless to the ecstasy of your own open heart, free and alive, passionate and expansive. An open heart steps onto the precipice of Life and fearlessly drops its petals onto the earth, dispersing its pollen into the wind, and fully and utterly surrenders to the whole, to the One.

The open heart knows no 'other' and recognizes All That Is as Itself. The open heart is Love, unknown to most who walk in flesh who cling to the concepts that keep us separate, small and afraid. It is Love, that cannot be altered or distorted by the mind. An open heart is Love. It is the Love we seek. And, when felt, for even a fleeting moment, we feel the freedom that is our true home, and we walk the earth yearning to return to that home of our open heart.

27

Compassion

COMPASSION IS A FEELING, AN e-motion that moves us into connection with another who is suffering. Compassion dares to wade in the water of suffering to touch the one who is submerged, unsure of whether or not she will drown. Compassion caresses her and sits with her in the watery depths of despair, breathing with her and for her, as it keeps its head above water. Compassion is fearless in its willingness to be present in the pain. It knows its connection to Divine sustenance and takes that knowing with it when it enters the confused state of human disconnection. Compassion leans into the dark hole of forgetfulness, connecting to what is human in order to bring together the one who weeps with the world of infinite love and wisdom. Compassion sits comfortably with the sadness and holds the bereaved gently. It opens the human heart to hold the fullness of her sweet pain and transforms it into the Love that it truly is. Compassion is the human expression of Divine Love. It is the delicious connection to humanity and sensation. Compassion is what binds us to each other. It offers the visceral awareness that we are truly One.

The challenge with compassion arises when we unconsciously choose compassion over alignment with Source. While compassion delivers us to the heart and soul of human connection, if we are not awake in our empathy, we may drown in our perception of another's pain. We may forget not only their intrinsic well-being that lies at the core of all beings, but we may also be swept away in the current of their disconnection, risking our own stability. This is the very thing necessary to support them in their resurfacing and realignment with their True Self. We must temper our propensity to dive into the depths of someone else's despair when our nature leans towards compassion and remember to keep our head above water.

I notice that, when I am feeling lost and unaligned, the peaceful, strong energy of my mother, my husband or my friend is much more comforting than someone who commiserates with me in my story of pain. Yet, I do not want them to pull me out of my emotions with the likes of a cheerleader on the sidelines, coaxing me to joy prematurely. I am grateful when they step into my space with love and reverence for the process I am experiencing—when they honor my pain, but do not join it. I am grateful when they sit quietly as I weep, and yet I can still feel their deep knowing that I am well, that I will feel well again, even when it seems impossible to me at that moment.

I choose to cultivate this perfect blend between the compassion that dares to lean into the heart of human suffering and the mindfulness of staying awake and connected. While reaching into this space of dark beauty, I remain grounded in knowing the well-being of the other and myself. I choose to be intimate with life, with my human nature, and I choose to be fiercely committed to aligning with my Divine nature. As I continue the practice of Unconditional Love, I am confident that my ability to remain in alignment, while compassionately connecting with another who is not, will grow and blossom.

28

Social Activism, Sacred Activism

I GREW UP IN A HOME where social activism was practiced, spearheaded by my father and his deep love and commitment to his family, the human family and the precious planet we inhabit. Recently, my father, who is now in his eighties, told me he wondered what it would be like when he dies. As we spoke I was surprised that he had not given it more thought. On the other hand, I have been fascinated with the world beyond this one and what lies in the realms of nonphysical since I was a teenager. I have read a lot of material that explores the spiritual world and life after death. My father shared that he felt there is simply too much to consider right here right now on this planet, pertinent issues at hand. His focus has been on how to make this world a better place. He is passionate about his role in affecting change in *this* physical realm.

I respect my father very much for this. I was exposed to a lot of alternative perspectives on social issues and politics as a result. I am sure that is why I never took anything at face value and often questioned the status quo. Free thinking was admired and modeled in my family. So it was not surprising when I made choices regarding childbirth, parenting, health and spirituality that were far from traditional.

However, my Dad's particular approach to social change was not mine. I wanted it to be, and I felt in some way that I might be disappointing him, because I did not share in his passionate desire to fight for human rights. He never said anything to make me feel that way and has always expressed great enthusiasm and appreciation for what I do as an artist and a mother. He recognizes the importance of my 'work' as valuable and has expressed his appreciation of my 'wisdom'. Yet, something has lingered within me from my youth that says that I wish I had the voice, the courage and the desire to get up amongst others to protest and organize, or at the very least, be informed of the injustices of the world. I have not always felt comfortable with my 'inaction' in an activist-oriented paradigm.

I believe that my fear of public speaking manifested when I was very young. My mother says that it was hard for me to get a word in edgewise when I was young, and she and my father created a signal for Dad when he would forget to include me in the conversation. I was a sensitive, pensive and emotional child. I have always taken things in deeply, and just in the last year, have been getting better at filtering and protecting myself from draining energies. The best way for me to describe it is that I often feel as though I have antennae all over my body, picking up on all the energies around me. The way I have dealt with this is to limit my interactions mostly to environments and people that do not drain me so much and to avoid news and other TV programs that cause me discomfort. I am very selective as to what I ingest with regards to both my body and my mind. My emotional guidance offers me immediate feedback on the information that I take in, letting me know if it is 'healthy' for me or not. Of course, to not be abreast of what is happening in the world is the antithesis of my father's approach to life.

I feel that my throat chakra became shut down fairly early on, even before I became aware of my fear of public speaking. This chakra is the energy center in the neck and shoulders area. The gift of this chakra is accepting your originality, expressing your authentic voice and speaking your truth. My dad is a speaker and a retired professor. My mother and Nana are both eloquent speakers as well, and both have been very passionate about social justice. Two of my sisters are performers and have woven their social activism in their own art forms in very powerful and vocal ways. I remember, when I was young, watching films of some of the atrocities that were occurring at the time in Central America and just wanting to weep. My heart would break, and my throat would close. The emotion was so encompassing that my voice was muffled by an unhealthy, disconnected form of compassion. I took on the pain of those whose stories were being told. It was and still is not productive when I go where I can no longer feel my own alignment.

I remember taking my father's class at the University of Windsor when I was just sixteen or seventeen years old. He showed a series of films about war and the devastating effects they were having on the communities involved. While I do not remember details of the class now, I do remember the feeling of being struck mute by this rising well of emotion and sadness that I felt after watching the documentaries. This sadness was not productive for me. It felt more like hopelessness. For my father, it fueled his passion toward action. For me, it made me feel paralyzed, and coupled with my desire to do what is right as perceived by my father, I felt inadequate in my inaction. He expressed frustration with the students, in our lack of participation and dialogue about the issues raised. I felt embarrassed and inwardly pressured and disappointed in myself for not being more vocal and articulate.

In retrospect, I have come to realize the connection between my debilitating fear to speak publicly about the things that I feel passionate about, my art, my spiritual path, or anything else that I want to share, and the shutting down that occurred during my youth as a result of my feelings of inadequacy in comparison to my father and other family members. I was focused on my desire for approval from my father. It is amazing how a limited thought pattern like that can take hold in our bodies and our minds for decades, casting a mesmerizing spell on us and burying its origin somewhere in our unconscious.

Fear can be so deeply ingrained within our vibration, that even if we have released our fear around the original event, similar events can trigger that fear in us again and again. For me, it happened whenever I wanted to speak to a group of people. A terrible physical sensation would sweep through my body: my heart would pound violently in my chest, I would sweat and tremble, my throat area would constrict, I would have shortness of breath and my head would throb. Although I knew I had the ability to express what I had to say, and others did not intimidate me, this physical reaction could be so intense that it would shut me down. On top of that, it was very difficult to maintain a train of thought with all of those physical conditions distracting me. I simply would not accept speaking engagements, because it was not worth the agonizing torment.

My self-expression and creativity found its home in painting. The first painting I created while living in Nassau was a malnourished boy from Ethiopia. I called it *Social Statement* and gave it to my father. I continued painting images of impoverished children, depictions of child labor and people from third world countries. It became a way to share the voice of concern my father had for these issues. My real voice with my art emerged, however, when I left the intellectual mind behind and opened to the language of my heart and gave my spirit a voice. As I developed my own relationship to life, independent of my parents, this spiritual voice found itself in my paintings. I always wrote copiously in journals, processing and contemplating, poetry flowing, and epiphanies recorded. It was personal though, just for me. The art was bold and loud, and yet did not require me to speak. It was natural and easy, and the process allowed me to tap into my Divine connection.

In my path to unraveling the elements within me that have kept me from being fully free, this issue of 'public speaking' would keep rearing its gnarly head. It was undeniable that I wanted to be liberated from this severe limitation. This fear felt somewhat like an anomaly as I grew into my sense of self and gained confidence. I was caught in a web of fear caused by unconscious thoughts that had developed from misperceptions I had made in my youth. I suspect this fear could have begun even further back and been part of my past lives as well. I could not seem to shake it. Just in the last year, I have worked with the flower essences to help with this and began to see a shift within a few months. I even accepted two speaking engagements and felt excited about the opportunity to share!

I am now honoring my way and my path. It may be different from my father's and from those like him who struggle for justice and peace, but in my own way, I am also trying to find creative solutions to help transform our world and the people upon it. My father works on the conditions, while I work on the vibration. This is the path that is most natural for me. It is the path that allows me to feel the flow of the Universe move through me and into all that I do, all that I create, and all the interactions that I have with others . . . when I am in that place of alignment. I have come to understand, not just intellectually, but viscerally, that this is an offering that is transformative, and while it works on the subtle body, it affects a core vibration that I can sense, when I'm sensitive to it.

Like my Dad, I believe that we are all interconnected, that the well-being of another affects the well-being of the whole. He sees it from a very tangible perspective of economics and social harmony in communities. I agree, and I also see it as an Ultimate truth that We Are All One. It is on my license plate . . . WERALL1. Not only are we a part of the human family, but we are also literally vibrational energy originating from the One Source, manifested in physical form. We are spiritual beings, divine in nature, experiencing ourselves as separate for the purpose of experience and expansion of the whole universe

My social activism is sacred activism, and while it may seem personal, it is far-reaching. For when we see through the eyes of Oneness, we recognize that self-service is service to the whole, just as selfless service is service to the self.

This is the sacred work of lightworkers. Lightworkers are those beings who practice mindfulness, meditation and energy healing. They are the artists, musicians, dancers, painters, poets and writers who work on a vibrational level to raise the energy of the whole. They inspire us to glimpse our True Nature, so that we may act from this place that is aligned with the power of the Universe.

When more of us are inspired to this powerful point of attraction, then conscious creation becomes more prevalent, and the conditions of our physical world reflect the inner world of those creating it. We are the creators of our own realities. Collectively, we, in our human form, are creating collective reality. All the beauty and horror of this planet are created and experienced by all of us inhabiting it, not just by our actions, but by our unconscious or deliberate thoughts. I believe that most of our creating has been by default, because we have not recognized how vital we are to the creation of our life or our experiences, personally and collectively.

My responsibility is to start with me, with my thinking. If I am at war in my mind, then how can I affect peace in the world around me? When I find peace within, then there is a chance to create it in my physical experience and inspire it in the hearts and minds of those around me. This inner work can have a powerful and rippling effect on the outer world. My activism is from the inside out. It is the only way I know how to do this. When I focus on desperate and complicated conditions outside of myself, I am laid out, emotionally depleted, anxious, confused, and in my paralysis, I often feel guilty and ashamed that I am not more proactive. Needless to say, this is neither aligned with Love, with God nor with what I know to be true about myself and humanity. It is a far cry from the Unconditional Love that I aspire to accomplish.

I am deeply grateful for the many paths that express and lead us back to our Divine nature. I deeply honor the many unique paths of the social activists, and the ways they affect positive change in our inner and outer worlds. I love the way my dad works passionately towards the elevation of the human race and his way of inspiring others to be more mindful of our beautiful planet and more loving to each other. He has inspired me to be the activist that I am, and now I accept that my way is equal, in value, to his.

My style of activism goes to the core of the mind, heart and spirit of humanity and unravels one limiting thought at a time, unlocking the gate to our own Divine Self. We all yearn for the balance, love and harmony that this connection to the Divine can bring. When I recognize that we are One, than each thought I unravel in me unravels in you. I am a vibrational elevator.

I am passionately committed to raising the vibration of humanity, starting with me. I am committed to Peace, Joy, Unconditional Love and Authenticity and practice it through mindful awareness in each moment. It is an active practice that requires an alert commitment to consciousness, to avoid being lulled back into habitual patterns of thought that continue to hold us all captive in the illusory world of fear, harboring thoughts of lack, loss, defensiveness, hurt and disconnection.

I am committed to take the high watch while you slumber, and when you awaken, we will awaken together to the magnificence of Who We Are and celebrate this grand and epic journey. All is well!

29

Prayer to Humanity

I WILL TAKE THE HIGH WATCH.
When you are weak,
I will be strong and know your strength.
When you have doubt,
I will know and trust.
When you are hungry,
I will see your fullness,
full of the sustenance that your heart desires,
that when realized,
feeds all hunger of the mind and the body.
When you have lost hope,
I will carry the torch of fire into the darkest caves of your
mind.
I will be that Light that you are, that I am.
I will see the truth of You

when you cannot.

I will not go to your place of hopelessness,
and I will not share words of comfort that skim the surface of
your mind,
barely grazing the heart of your yearning.
I will walk in the Truth of your well-being,
knowing your Divine nature,
your brilliant illumined Self,
seeing it,
feeling it,
breathing it
into every cell of my being.
I will blaze through the illusion of your limitedness
and sink into the rich depth of your sweet courage,
fearless and free.

You, the One who chose this grand adventure
to expand and experience Life,
regardless of the perceived perils that forgetfulness invokes,
the illusive veil of amnesia that we all chose as we came
forth,
knowing the power of its spell
that offers us this diverse stage of experience
for the pure joy of expansion . . .
the contractions of this veiled reality
propelling us beyond where
anyone has ever been before.

I will hold the high watch
when you are lost in the illusion
And when this blessed veil of forgetfulness

blinds you beyond recognition,
I will see the truth of you.
When your heart and mind is shrouded in the darkness of
fear,
when your anger and spite consumes you,
I will stay seated in the shrine of remembrance,
focused on your Divinity.
I will not go where you go
when despair is your companion,
because I know the truth.
I know you.
I know you,
for you are me.
We are one.

I will hold the high watch.
Stay Awake
and feel, know and express
the freedom, clarity, joy, peace, love, well-being that we are.
I will live it,
breathe it,
speak it,
experience it.

And with this sustained vigilance
of tireless wakefulness,
I will inspire you to know what I know,
and you will be drawn to the flame of your own brilliance.
I promise
I will keep that flame burning hot and big and steady,
so that when you are ready,
you cannot miss it.

Bare Beauty

The heat and light will be so compelling
that even the Veil of Forgetfulness
will not shroud your remembering,
and we will know our Oneness once again.

So, for now, as you slumber and as you awaken,
I promise
to hold the high watch
for myself and for you,
for I have had enough sleep for ten thousand lifetimes.

30

DENIAL: Stuck in the Birth Canal

M Y COMMUNITY, AND PERHAPS THE whole country, has been shaken to its core. Nine praying parishioners, in the historic black church, Mother Emmanuel African Methodist Episcopal Church, in Charleston, SC, were murdered by a twenty-one-year-old white man/child who felt he needed to kill them, because they were black.

My body aches, my skin is vibrating and my chest is heavy. I fluctuate from grief to anger to fear to hurt to peace to confusion and back all over again. This ubiquitous issue of racism in America, which always simmers beneath the surface, feels like it has exploded in a crescendo that cannot be ignored.

Over the past several years, there has been a growing movement here in the United States: Black Lives Matter. Through this movement, people are working together towards validating the lives of black people. It was created in response to the acquittal of George Zimmerman, the murderer of Trayvon Martin, a seventeen-year-old black boy who, like so many before him and after him, was profiled, targeted and killed just because of his color. There has been a growing awareness of police brutality towards black people, particularly black males. By spotlighting these incidents, widely available now through the advent of social media, the nation is becoming more aware of the institutionalized racism that has existed for almost four hundred years, post-slavery. Significant progress has been made, in so many ways. This very progress has made it possible for me, as a biracial, black woman, artist, shop owner and mother, to be in denial about the festering wound that continues to usurp the vitality and true freedom that I seek in my individual life.

I am at a point in my process where I'm experiencing a long, painful, almost unbearable contraction. I want so badly to call out for an epidural to numb the pain that is arising within me. I am not only ready to numb out, but I am also ready to run from the responsibility for that which is about to be born! Yet, I have prepared my whole life for this very moment to stay awake and conscious through this unbearable pain. I have practiced and studied the art of allowing and the beauty of breath and the essential need for authenticity. I refuse to let the brutal death of these nine beautiful beings, from my own community, be in vain. I may not be able to change the conditions that are out of my control. However, I can go within myself and attempt to look at my part in the Denial that perpetuates the sickness of this collective consciousness of which I am a part. I may not be able to get all white people to do the work, to admit to their own part in this Denial or for all black people to look at how they may participate in self-degrading consciousness that keeps them shackled and oppressed, but I can do the work to look at it in myself. I may not be able to get the lawmakers to change the way they treat my black brothers, sisters and children, but I can begin to change the way I do. I can begin to check the ways in which I participate in the collective perception and treatment of the very race I call my own.

There is no turning back now. The baby of freedom, deep love and brutal honesty has been conceived. It is too late to abort the undeniable presence of this New Way, but this baby of collective yearning is no walk in the park. She/he has not come forth to allow us to stay in the comfort of our air-conditioned denial. She/he is here to take us back into the sticky, hot wetness of the South Carolina marshlands, into the fields where my great-great-great white granddaddy slave master laid with my great-great-great enslaved grandmother enough times for her to give birth to thirteen babies, the color of my light brown skin.

> There is no turning back now from becoming the mother to this child of freedom.

> *"Breathe. Feel. Allow. Breathe. Feel. Allow."*

> *"Don't give up, sweet sister of the flesh. You can birth this child that will ravish the earth with her/his unabashed, uncensored, unleashed, raw freedom, unwilling to be defined by anything that is not pure Love. Not the kind of love that behaves in ways that are appropriate and palatable, but the kind of love that is fearless to speak its truth, the kind of love that risks death to dive into the heart of dysfunction, unconsciousness and denial, and expose it for all to see."*

201

"Breathe. Feel. Allow."

"You will be okay. You can do this. You are not your body—your body is yours!"

Tears slipping down brown cheeks, sweat rolling down tense back, between breasts, thighs.

"Breathe."

Deep guttural groans, opening the dark cavernous canal. Eyes closed, heart thumping, body trembling uncontrollably.

"God is here. Undeniably. God is here. It feels like I am going to die. My back feels like it will break. My insides are tearing apart! How can I do this?! It is impossible!"

Whispers fill my ear . . . *"But God is here. Let go!"*

I get quiet, so I can hear the compelling tone of a whisper.

"God is here. Surrender, and you will be delivered."

It is almost inaudible, yet peace floods me, and the air is still in the soundless suspension of time. I want to hear. I want to feel the peace on the wings of the whisper.

I listen, waiting . . .

"God is in the fire, in the flesh, in the anger and in the peace. God is in the silence, in the screams, in the darkness and in the light. You cannot not be with God. There is nothing God is not!"

Listen . . .

"God is in the movement, in the stillness.

God is flesh in you and in every other speck of life.

God longs for you,

As you long for God.

God is the child you are birthing, who is unafraid to wreak havoc on your life,

so you and God and All That Is can expand."

Listen . . .

Whispering softly,

"You can mother this child, sweet sister of the flesh. Be brave. You know how to do this. We have prepared you. You have done this before."

Resistance arising . . .

"But I don't want to spiral into postpartum hell. I don't want the responsibility of a child that burns the village of false comfort. I am scared shitless!"

Breath held, body tight, chest contracted, legs held together . . . tight. Numb pain. Fear. Chest aching. Heart pounding. Throat closed.

"Breathe . . ."

I can barely hear. I am drowning. The baby is stuck in the birth canal, and I am drowning!

"Breathe!"

It is louder now. The still numb pain is worse than the other kind of pain that seems to propel the baby forth. I am ready to scream, yell, push, allow, breathe, cry, sweat, wait, listen, shake, wail—whatever it takes to get this heavy weight off my chest that is crushing me with fear.

Deep breath! I can breathe now. Still shaking. But oxygen floods in, and the baby is moving through flesh like a lightning bolt. My heart feels like it is going to break through my chest.

"Focus. Breathe. I can do this. I have done this before. I am an eternal being. I am not my body! My body is mine."

Peace.

The baby is imminent but not yet born. I am in limbo.

I am the laboring mother, and I am the fearless one, about to be born into flesh. I am the mother of flesh and the spirit of Source. Like Mother Emmanuel Church, who has held the martyred victims of racism and the child of systemic racism in the form of the killer within the womb of history, I am that mother who labors and gives birth to the victim and the villain.

"How can I mother this self, so that she/he can be a full expression of the True Self, the Divine Self that is centered in freedom, love and joy?"

The whisper is back:

"Honesty, faith, vulnerability, courage, surrender. Be willing to crack open and feel the pain once anesthetized by a nation, not yet ready for this Awakening. Awakening is at hand. The time is now and never was before and never will be again. Now. You will be guided."

"As the killer was at the tip of a mountain of collusion and denial that brewed him into existence, so are you at the point of power that is at the tip of a mountain of momentum that is fueled by the focused realms of Divine Guidance. It is a mountain of love, born of the blood and tears of the ancestors whose sweat watered the hot fields of the South, the ones who endured the Middle Passage of the Atlantic Slave Trade, and those who chose death over bondage."

205

"You and the people of your community, of your time, of your country, are called to the top of this mountain with the infinite resources of the Universe holding you, as you give birth to the freedom that is your birthright! Do not be afraid of this wild child, this free-spirited one, that begs to be born through you. It is what you have wanted, what you have always wanted. This child will show you how to be its mother. Do not be afraid. You are ready. You have prepared for lifetimes to bring forth this One who knows Its Oneness, who is flagrantly free. This One will lead the way, and all that is needed is faith the size of a mustard seed to allow for the redemption of your indentured soul to know once again the smell of freedom. Those who have been incarcerated by their fear of losing the safe refuge, created at the expense of the freedom of others, and those who have been shackled by a self-loathing, born of the dehumanization of a race they were born into, will be free. All yearn for this freedom. The collective contraction is underway. Align with Love, and the labor will be less arduous. All will Awaken. All will be redeemed, renewed and re-membered."

I received/channeled this writing while in my Akashic Records.

31

RACE and RADICAL HONESTY

I AM BORN OF THE FLESH of a white man, a social activist, a sensitive, intellectual white man. I am born of the flesh of a black woman, a social change agent, a bridge for different ways and different races, an artist and a spiritual seeker.

I have benefited from my light brown skin and my "exotic" appearance by being able to safely step into a world where black people were once tortured and enslaved. With my palatable demeanor and image, it is easy for white people to discount my blackness and embrace the familiar part of me, which keeps them feeling safe and comfortable. I have benefited from this privilege of not being 'too black' in a world that subliminally is terrified of the wrath of the black man, a white world that its own ancestors enslaved.

I opened a business on Broad Street on the edge of the wealthiest part of old Charleston and have made a living selling beauty to mostly white women. I have known that the maleness and blackness of my own husband, and business partner, could threaten the comfort of some women I serve, and he is aware that he must tread carefully in their presence, for we rely on their patronage to feed the mouths of our three black sons. I am aware that when my brown-skinned husband gets out of our Volvo SUV, even though we have the privilege of a nice car, he does not have the privilege of being seen as nice and safe, as white women sometimes cling to their purses and run across the street for fear of him. Yet, she would not be afraid of me, I assure you.

Yes, I benefit from white privilege too. I do not know what it is to be a black man in America. I do, mind you, know what it is for the black men I love, for my husband of over thirty years and my twenty-two-year-old son. It breaks my heart to witness the double standard they experience and the fear America has of my precious, gentle men.

Still, I struggle with my own judgment and prejudice about the black urban style that perpetuates stereotypical images that threaten my son's safety. I fear that the white world in which we live will not see him for who he really is. I have subscribed to the necessities of decorum and cringe when his pants 'sag' and when his grammar is not the 'Queen's English'. I want him to behave in a way that is palatable, like me.

I have been in denial that a deep ache resides within me and when the issue of race arises, I want to run, minimize, or spiritualize into a place of comfort, before I am able to acknowledge and heal the ugliness lurking in the dark, cobwebbed corners of my uninvestigated mind. I have denied my white side when matters of racial divisiveness arise, choosing the side of the 'victim', rather than aligning with the ugliness of white superiority.

208

I grew up in a white world where I felt inferior to my white classmates and superior to my black ones, although there were very few in my eight years of elementary school in Canada. I felt unattractive and insecure. Of course, this was subconscious for a while, but with adolescence, the awareness of my identity and self-image grew. I realized that I did not fit the image of beauty portrayed in popular culture. The 'exotic' images of the light-skinned black woman came later. The feeling of 'less than' steeped into me like an insidious, undetected disease. It corroded my self-esteem as I quietly and secretly held this conflicting feeling of superiority/inferiority, something I would never speak aloud, because it felt icky, shameful and confusing.

Thank God for my fearless, freedom-seeking mother, who chose to move to the Bahamas, where I was able to join her and my sister a year later. It was pivotal in restoring my self-esteem and self-love, allowing me to feel love for others in a way that was not possible before this transformation. I could not have imagined what it would mean for me to live in a black country and go to a 'black' school, to be in the majority at such a tender age, when self-identity is being formed.

But before this transformation could occur, I experienced a huge contraction when my mother and sister left me in Canada, without the balance of my black mother to temper the self-loathing that arose from the part of me that wanted to be white, to fit in, and to be pretty like 'them'. I am sure that it did not seem so bad to others, but the pain and anger I felt inside and did my best to suppress, at times, felt suffocating. I did not understand it as I do now. I was terribly confused, as I suppose many adolescent children are. For me, race was a part of that confusion.

When on vacation, I thought people would look at me and

my three other biracial siblings and assume we were adopted, since my Dad and Stepmother were both white. Ironically, my brother *was* adopted, but I wanted to claim the blood of my father. He was mine, and I belonged to him.

Then Alex Haley's movie *Roots* came out, and we sat night after night watching the TV series that portrayed the unspeakable history of slavery in one man's family tree. It was an unprecedented look at slavery, never-before-seen on TV. Sarah and I would begin each night nestled up under each arm of our beloved father, the social activist, who wanted to share this historical and important look at slavery with his children who came from this heritage. Sadly, he shared with us later, that while we watched the show, we would begin to slide away from his warm embrace. Subconsciously, we must have connected him with the hideous and oppressive behavior of the white men portrayed in the saga of slavery—our mother, symbolizing the black women raped by the slave masters and spat upon by the white women, became the victim. In that moment, I did not want to claim the white blood of my father. I was only eleven years old, and Sarah was only twelve at that time.

This is how insidious the culture of racism is. And no, it is not confined just to the soil of the United States. It is all-pervasive, and forms of racism affect the self-perception and sense of dignity of people all over the globe. Certainly, Canada is not exempt from this Western portrayal of beauty and the distorted perception of blackness in our culture. American culture is the seat of Western civilization, which has stretched its influence all over the globe.

I feel that the process of healing this gaping chasm and festering wound of racism begins with radical honesty. And so, I step into this precarious and vulnerable ground of racial honesty, through self-reflection, joining the ranks of others who have done so for eons. I call upon the strength of my ancestors, both black and white, who have been conscious and unconscious perpetrators or victims in this long and oppressive history. I call upon the wisdom and perspective of the Divine that now engulfs the collective mind of those who have returned to the Soul of God, no longer encumbered by human identities —identities that we, here on earth, are challenged to reimagine, so that we can expand from the compressed place that racism has caused.

Radical honesty must precede radical acceptance. Until we admit that there *is* sickness, we simply cannot *begin* to allow for the healing that is necessary. It takes courage to be radically honest and recognize our own part in the denial that keeps us stuck both on a personal and collective level. Until we fully feel that which we have buried, suppressed, ignored, denied, or numbed, we will not be able to experience the freedom and peace that comes with radical acceptance.

While I cannot control what others do or be, or the abhorrent conditions that show up in our world, I can choose to do this deep, inner work of radical honesty, with a willingness to feel what comes up to be felt and healed.

I feel that this is a crucial step, not only to uproot the systemic tentacles of racism, but also the many oppressive systems that threaten humanity and the delicate balance of all life on this precious planet. Once we take this step we will be able to experience the unfolding of Radical Acceptance that is at the core of a liberated mind and a liberated society. The kind of acceptance that resists nothing, and fearlessly opens to all that arises, to give birth to a New Way.

Once I liberate my own mind, I have a chance at the freedom and joy and kind of love that is so intimate that *every* face I encounter is a reflection of my Beloved. *Even* when it is the face of the killer, who, in his ignorance, fueled a revolution of change that is awakening us to our collective disease.

I embrace the contrast, the contraction, and the pain. I embrace the human part of me that resists, knowing it is the price I must pay to be part of the brilliant expansion of the Universe. I am willing to risk the resistance contained within the human perspective, and the pain it provokes, so that I may experience the process of Awakening, again and again, to the truth of Oneness and the bare beauty that is at the core of all things.

I have given birth to the fearless, flagrantly free-spirited-One.

It has come forth, and I lay worn and hungry, sore and exhausted.

I still tremble and await the contractions that proceed birth, to dispel the afterbirth,

the remnants that sustained this liberated Soul, so that he/she could inhabit

the body of God

right here on Earth once more.

I have faith that I will be able to mother and nurture and one day even let go of this Free One, in a way that will allow her/him to stay free and fearless.

In the meantime I am ravenous!

32

Faith in the Darkness

"A flower has the good sense to turn its face to the sun and relish warmth and sunlight on each petal. But the flower also has the good sense to explore the dark, confining earth, the deepest, blackest space, and draw sustenance from that."
-Joseph

I LOVE THE LIGHT AND ALL that feels good. Who would not want to feel good? It feels good to feel good. I love the way the light enlivens me to action, inspires me and activates a deep sense of joy within me, and . . . I love the darkness that allows my weary body and mind to rest when the active energy of the sun recedes to another part of the planet. I love the dark rich soil that nourishes and brings forth life, like the womb of the mother. I love the way the darkness allows me to see the light of the moon, the way it defines that which is light.

Darkness and light are a part of each other. They belong

215

to each other. I desire to embrace the darkness more fully and gently release my resistance to all that is not light and 'beautiful' and comfortable. I want to be willing to accept *all* of life as it arises in my own experience. I want to be able to have faith that what shows up in my life is offered by my Soul, to expand, grow and evolve, whether it feels good or not. Sometimes the feeling of 'not good' is really the resistance to what is. It is the indicator that I am out of alignment with Source, which sees all that is as fully acceptable. It is my resistance to what is that creates the feeling of suffering, rather than the presence of the 'unlovable' reality, which comes forth for my opening.

Radical Acceptance is the ultimate stance of nonresistance. It is Unconditional Love. It is a deep awareness that all is lovable and that I have enough room within my consciousness to accept and love the darkness as much as I do the light. When I am able to do this, I am re-membered. I become whole again. For the dark and light are one. They define each other. One gives form to the other. Instead of pushing against and pulling away from the darkness that threatens to engulf me, I choose to face it and gently lean into it, so I may be nourished by the pain it elicits.

When I was experiencing the most intense 'contraction,' when Chaz was hospitalized, I slipped into a deep, dark hole of heartbreak and fear that threatened to crush the life out of me. All attempts to hold on to control were futile. Years of worry and mental strategizing, in an attempt to keep him safe from his own recklessness, gave way to the dark cavernous pain that lived beneath my attempts to control the uncontrollable. At first, the suffering was unbearable, and I thought I might lose my mind, the very thing we feared we might have lost in our son.

As days went by and we watched for signs of 'sanity' to

emerge in him, I noticed that the confined space within the darkness was beginning to become a welcome refuge from the blaring light of life. I grew aware of a collective consciousness, the heart of humanity, living within the warm, black, fertile soil of darkness. What seemed flat, lifeless and scary at first, became luscious in its blackness, and soon I could sense the variations of shade and color that were more diverse in beauty than I could ever have imagined. I could not avoid the darkness that was at the threshold of this unbearable pain, so I looked into it, and its rich wholeness was revealed to me. I realized that it was holding me up, keeping me from the complete collapse that seemed imminent. And yet, as my knees buckled beneath me, the darkness, drenched in the tears of all those who surrendered to grief, became the very sustenance I needed at that time.

I envision myself buried in the earth, being held up by walls of dark, moist, warm soil, oxygen entering through my pores, embraced by the womb of the Mother, sustained by her love and nurtured by her compassion. She has held the pain of all humanity, and in her all-encompassing heart, and in her sweet nourishing soil, she has absorbed and transformed our sorrow for our reaping. For as the seeds of our pain grow, from the willingness to surrender to this vast reservoir of Love and Guidance, we reap the harvest of a newly expanded consciousness.

It was my experience then, and in all the moments when I have surrendered to pain, that the most beautiful and delicious fruit of this labor awakened my own compassion and connection with life and humanity. The human condition offers the rich opportunity to experience the contrast in a way that allows for the expansion of life. It is the darkness that is the result of light casting shadows that gives dimension and beauty to this physical life we have chosen. The experiences we consider dark are the very ones that render life so precious. Without the looming promise of death, would life be as meaningful, as revered? Death is akin to darkness. It is the void of what is known, and yet, if we allow ourselves to venture occasionally into the darkness, which we have been so fervently taught to avoid, we may become more familiar and comfortable with the abstract nature of death and the gift it provides. Possibly, we could enter into our own death experience or witness the death of others with more ease, acceptance, presence and love.

It is the alchemy of pain that the darkness elicits. My grief and hurt, disappointment and hopelessness, which were born of the Emmanuel Massacre, gave way to a powerful time of inner transformation and collective Awakening. The grief was nurtured within the compassionate Mother, and when I allow myself to fully feel the pain, then the alchemy must surely follow. It is when we suppress our grief that we become stuck in the birth canal and movement is slow and agonizing. It is the avoidance of what is and of the emotions that beg to be felt that keep us in the darkness longer than our Soul intended. I feel awakened to a more human, compassionate Self. I feel lighter for having delved into the darkness of despair. I feel more willing to lean into the parts of life that I have shied away from in order to feel safe and happy. I feel stronger. I feel less afraid to cross the threshold into authenticity, which threatens to rock my boat of comfort and propriety.

I am grateful for the sweet breath of death that surrenders us to the Divine and gives meaning and depth to this life we live. I am grateful for the alchemy achieved by the fated tragedy, which is opening minds and hearts in the most fascinating way; each of us processing this Awakening in our own unique way. I am grateful for the dimension and complexity that has been revealed about our community and society as a result of this painful reckoning, and I am grateful for the opportunity for healing that being transparent has offered me.

As I ponder the emotions and thoughts that have arisen, I realize that a new humility has been born within me. I have been inspired into deeper self-reflection and a desire to uproot limited patterns of thought from my subconscious, through this process of looking head-on at racism, prejudices and judgments, which have been festering in the collective mind, and to some degree within mine, which keeps us separate from each other, and ultimately, from God.

It is liberating and profoundly unifying to walk into the darkness of grief, marinating in its fermenting ache, until it is ripe and ready for the light to cast away all shadows of sorrow and reveal the Divine within all humanity. I am more deeply aware of the value of this marination process, so that the fullness of feeling can be felt, allowing me the opportunity to savor the most delicious experiences life has to offer, which are rich, dark, velvety, smooth, crunchy, sweet, sour, creamy, light, fluffy and everything in between.

When we deny the darkness and all that it represents, we deny the dark, warm womb from which our very flesh was born; we deny the mystery, the void, the unknown, the future, the infinite realm of possibility; we deny the night; we deny the ending that is not only imminent but essential for our expansion and the expansion of All. When we deny the darkness, we not only deny the human condition, we deny the Divine that lives beyond our eyes that need light to see.

To cultivate a relationship with the darkness, we must have faith. Faith is often born of surrender, sometimes forced by the human conditions of life that take us to our knees. Faith is an empty concept until we are truly enshrouded in darkness. Then, and only then, when we call out for help, do we know the deep, sweet comfort of belonging to the darkness . . . *and* the light.

33

HUMILITY

THOUGHTS HAVE BEEN RACING THROUGH my mind. So many words, ideas, concepts and awarenesses are flowing through me, as though I am a river, without any say as to what flows into my waters. It has been an intense day for me. As I have listened to others process their emotions and experiences, I have been absorbing it all and attempting to decipher everything. I feel a titillating sensation of words yearning to be formed and placed on page. Yet, I wonder what form this expression will take at this time.

Humility is the word that inspired me to sit up from my prone position, reeling from a day of thoughts undefined. Humility—what does that mean? For me, it means recognition of the path as equal for each of us. Recognition that my unfolding is the unfolding and awakening of all, inspired by the all of us and offering Awakening to the all of us.

Humility is the temperament that I came forth to develop and cultivate for the unfolding of humanity, beginning with me. I came forth to remember my Oneness and in doing so, experience the Humility of being all of it—the imperfection and the perfection. I am not reaching for perfection. I am reaching for union with my Divine Self. To be one-minded with the Source version of me, so I can experience the freedom that comes with this perception. When I am in the Awakened Self, then there is infinite space for the previously resisted aspects of reality, those unacceptable conditions. The Awakened perception dissolves the individualized perceptions, and a non-dual reality arises that is utterly humble. It becomes One, not only with joy and freedom but with the valley of humanity that is unaware of its wholeness. In the Awakened mind, judgment falls away and so does the other—the apparent other dissolves into me. If I perceive that I am more evolved than another, I am not Awakened. The Awakened mind experiences no separation. Awakening is a process, because it is a continual evolution that cannot be realized until the mind of the whole is awake unto itself. Is that even possible? I don't know. But until the limited, restrictive thoughts of all of humanity are unraveled, then Awakening is an evolving process, unfolding in me, as them and as me.

I have become aware of the quiet and powerful quality of Humility, without feeling unworthy and without feeling that someone else knows better than I. At the same time, it is Humility that knows I do not know better than another. It is the Humility that holds Awareness as having the utmost importance and does not necessarily dance in the vibrational frequencies of another's disconnection but honors the process, recognizing the value of the contractions.

Humility tempers the human mind that seeks importance,

which separates itself from the awareness of our Oneness. Humility is a trait necessary only within the framework of the human mind, not in the Awakened mind that is One with Source, and thus, strives not to know its Oneness with All, because it is Awareness Itself, expressed in all ways, completely and utterly free from the human mind, which is mired in duality consciousness. It revels in the expression of the human consciousness as an opportunity for expansion.

Humility is like compassion. It keeps me connected to humanity, without keeping me *from* my Divine Self. It cultivates equanimity within me, allowing my alignment to affect the whole, because I am One with the whole. I am the Divine and the human. I am the Awakened mind, and I am the one who has forgotten my brilliance, desperate and blinded from what is ultimately True. I have lingered in the darkness that sustained me, and have grown within its fertile, rich soil of sunless moisture, stretching within time into the light-filled Awakening of Divine Oneness. I am grateful for the human perspective, which guides me back to the felt union with all of you. It is the most delicious journey to come back again and again to this brilliant Awakening, to the love affair with you all and with the I that I perceive myself to be in my human sense of otherness.

34

The Call to Love What Is

I WAS JUST SCROLLING THROUGH MY Facebook posts and read about the Bill being passed for the Confederate Flag to be removed from South Carolina's Statehouse grounds. In just a few days, the KKK, the notorious white supremacy group, will be marching at the Statehouse to protest. Seven black churches in the Southeast have been burned down since the killing of the Emmanuel Nine. All of this is happening in my own backyard.

The challenge of *loving what is* is daunting at times, and yet, I realize that it is the key to the liberation I seek. To love what is does not mean that I am comfortable with what is, or even that I like it. It does not mean that 'what is' is acceptable to me, but it does mean that I am able to practice radical acceptance and deep Unconditional Love that stretches beyond the confines of what I previously deemed unlovable. It is more about cultivating faith, a deep trust in life. It is more about my ability to embrace and appreciate the darkness and the vast dimension it contains. It is more about honoring what is, what shows up, as part of the divine process. Loving what is is about non-resistance, sweet surrender, opening my heart wide enough to hold all of life as God unfolding, expanding.

When I am able to hold this stance, Love flows like a river, unobstructed by man-made dams that attempt to control and manipulate the flow in ways that are unnatural to its current. When I am in this stance, I am able to breathe deep full breaths, so I can absorb the sustenance that is provided by the nourishing green life, abundant on this planet. Oxygen fills my lungs when I love what is, and I am not afraid of pollution, viruses or allergens. I am fearless and creative and inspired, when I love what is. I am more aware of the unfolding beauty and brilliant opening to life and see clearly the purpose of the contrast, the contractions, that deepen my relationship with the darkness, which nurtures and cradles me, preparing me for the expansion of Light—for I am the Light that is defined by the darkness.

To love what is is a radical position to take and will be misunderstood by many as complacent. However, when the reservoirs of life-force and vitality are released, when resistance is relinquished, then the true creative nature of our beings is free to flow without obstruction. Then we flow naturally down the current of our life, towards the desires we have defined as a result of living and contracting and dipping into the dark, deep spaces of the unknown. Held within the vast reservoir of desire that dwells at the base of our river, are our dreams of peace, freedom, joy, respect, love, health, abundance and ease, not just for ourselves, but also for those we love and for all of humanity.

When my nonresistant, free-flowing, loving-what-is self

rides the current of life into this cool pool of my divine creation, I experience the manifestations revealing themselves to me one by one. The exhilaration of these revelations propel me forth into the never-ending current of expansion, giving birth to more desires, more experiences, more contrast, more life-nurturing darkness and more life-expanding lightness.

When I love what is, complacency is not an option. I am too intimate and connected to life to be distant and uninterested. My heart aches for each succulent vision, each muffled sound, every last breath of a loved one, the caress of a gentle breeze on my skin, even the violence of hurricanes and thunder. My heart lies open to the brilliant beauty of each moment, present to all of it, all of the pain and sweetness that arises within and around me. I am willing to invite it all in, when I can, to be awake to this Love. When I love what is, I am accepting all of me, just as I am at that moment, even when I am lethargic, listless and afraid. I am able to sit in that energy and love it, as it restores me and summons me to desire something else. Without the resistance, I flow easily downstream and gently back into the feelings of vitality and peace. I may not be able to be completely free of the pain that life at times elicits, but I can be free of the suffering, which my resistant mind inflicts. In practicing Unconditional Love, Radical Honesty, Radical Acceptance and Loving What Is, I am cultivating an environment where suffering cannot flourish, and the blossoming of my own creations bloom prolifically in this Garden of Eden we call home.

When I love what is, I am not concerned about the faint filter that seems to have blurred my vision, as of late. I am not concerned about the churning in my stomach or the stabbing pains that occasionally force me to recline and groan for relief. I am not concerned about getting breast cancer because it runs in the family or worried about my son revisiting the world of insanity. I have faith when I love what is, faith that all is perfect and that the unfolding is at hand. I trust that God is present, even in the pain, the cancer and the son. I have faith in evolution, in movement, in change and in the darkness of the unknown. I have faith that there is redemption for the killers and the killed, the pillagers and the pillaged. When I love what is, I feel safe, because there is nothing that is not lovable.

When I am loving what is, I am unencumbered by fear and the need to control, so I am infinitely creative and deeply inspired, aligned with the Source of All of Life. Life beckons me. I follow with joy and ease. I do not pull back from life, for Love is fearless and intimate and inclusive. Love knows no boundaries and weeps not for loss, but for the opening of once closed hearts, succulent, red and raw. Love yearns to be devoured whole, like the body and blood of Christ, consumed for our wholeness.

To love what is is to see the solution in the problem, to know the lightness within the darkness. Love does not see a separation between the two. It knows that there is only One, and yet, it revels in the many. In our world of polarity, duality and illusive separation, it is deeply radical to love what is. It may seem to some that this is anti-compassionate, anti-action or blind acceptance. To me, it is the epitome of compassion that leans into the darkness, undaunted by the wailing pain of humanity. It is conscious, wide-awake acceptance, which flies in the face of conditional love. It is the very vibrational frequency that inspires the most powerful and creative action that is aligned with the Infinite reSource of the Universe.

Loving what is
is a Radical Awakening.

35

The Healer is Healed

HAVE YOU EVER FOUND YOURSELF arguing for your limitations, wanting the sympathy of others when you feel stuck, sick, uncomfortable or in pain? Do you ever feel the need to justify your condition to others, and when they are optimistic too quickly about the situation, you want to say to them, "Wait a minute, not so fast! I am not there yet. I want to be positive, and yes, I want to get out of this rut, this unwanted experience, but I am not there yet, and if you think I am, you may just leave me in the dust." Sometimes 'faking it till you make it' doesn't quite cut it. When you say to someone that you are feeling great, and the truth is your body is wrought with pain, and then maybe you feel you will not get the attention you need, both practically and emotionally. If you say, "I am financially fine," and you are scared shitless about where your next meal is going to come from, then you are not going to be able to attract the vibration of prosperity. Your human self may fear that the very help you need cannot reach you without them knowing that there is indeed a real need that must be addressed.

This dilemma is not a simple one. It can get a lot of folks in trouble, when they ignore the realness of their condition to focus only on the esoteric approach to attract a better condition. We must address the feelings that arise to be able to truly evolve from the current condition into a more expansive one. So if fear is awakened within you, do not run from it. Listen to it. What does it have to tell you? Then, very deliberately, soothe yourself back into alignment, not by ignoring the fear, but by acknowledging it, observing it and feeling it. Try to watch it from an objective stance, while being aware of the feeling. Notice the sensations within your body. Where does the fear live in you? Breathe deeply and stay present in the moment and in that feeling. Stay vigilantly present. When we are present, we are less likely to be in our thinking that causes the resistance, which is at the root of all suffering. Practice this presence like your life depends on it. Feel into your body. Notice the air and sounds around you. Feel the different energy centers in your body. Notice what you feel. Try not to judge the sensations with any thought process, and when you notice that happening, gently refocus your attention on the body.

Sometimes we deny what is present, because we think it should be different. We believe, if we focus on it, that we will create more of the same. "Thoughts held in mind, produce after their kind." This is a foundational belief of the new thought movement and those who follow the principles of 'The Law of Attraction.' The tricky aspect of this awareness is that many of us become afraid of our own thoughts that we know are limited and fearful. We are afraid we will attract the fruits of our worrisome and fearful thoughts that we seem to have no control over. This is certainly something I have felt, and I know many of my friends who believe in this powerful Law of Attraction, have felt this as well. It is somewhat of a paradox: while the knowledge of this Law offers an incentive to be mindful of what we allow ourselves to focus on, encouraging us to choose more consciously our thoughts and actions, it can also cause us to fear our own thoughts, compounding the problem many of us are grappling with.

So, I want to suggest a gentler approach. Focus less on the thoughts and more on the feelings. Let the feelings arise, and as I have already suggested, bring presence and awareness to the sensations. Allow what is to be present in the powerful transformational moment of the Divine Now. Everything that ever was and ever will be can only be experienced in the here and now. Thought forms can arise. These are often figments of our imagination, sometimes of a proposed future or a distorted perception of the past. It is too hard to come at it from the thought that indeed is creating our reality. It is like trying to put out a fire with more fire, fear with more fear. When we stop fighting or fleeing or resisting what is, we sink into the nectar of its offering. We have access to the Divine Source of All that Is!

When someone says to you, after or during a time that we have been struggling with some issue, "I am so glad you are doing better," notice the resistance to the words that may feel too optimistic too soon. Notice how it feels and where you feel it in your body. Breathe the life-giving energy of breath into your cells. When thoughts arise, simply notice if they are resisting or allowing the process of staying present.

I know that when those words were recently offered to me,

as I was experiencing intense physical discomfort and acute fear around the condition, I felt a little resistance. I wanted to say, "Wait! I am in the process. I don't feel better yet, but I will. I know I will. Stay with me where I am. Walk into the dark waters of the night, and wait with me there, so I am not alone while I heal. Sing me to sleep. Caress my cheeks, and remind me that I am safe."

I do not want to tell you that I am well and then you think, "Oh good. I don't have to worry about her. She is okay." I want you to ask, "Is there anything I can do to be present for you?"

How can we support each other, so we do not evoke the need for another to argue for their limitations? When one is in the midst of experiencing their limitations, they are not so strong in their ability to perceive the very thing that will release them from the pain. A new perspective must be born from those dark waters of gestation. The new perspective must come from the perceiver, not from the loved ones observing them.. So, where does that leave the loved ones? In the position to be the midwife, who reverently holds space, knowing deeply the well-being that is all pervasive. She does not prod or demand the birth before it is time, but aids only if life is stuck in the birth canal and more extreme measures are required.

It takes skill and awareness, which many do not have, to attend to the healing process of another. The lay midwife is trained in the healthy and natural birth process, so she is a master at innovating to assure this intention. The western medical model trains its doctors in the complications of birth; therefore, their focus is slanted toward focusing on what could possibly go wrong, rather than cultivating an environment and foundation for a natural and conscious birth process. Both models have their place, and I honor the work of both types of healers.

I feel it is time for the model of the midwife to find its home more rooted in the practices of our New Earth, as all of humanity becomes more awakened. It is the ancient way, and its wisdom is vast. Midwifery offers our society a crucial model of what it is for a healer to be present for others who are undergoing transition and expansion and for those who are in the throes of labor, both metaphorically and literally. I feel it is time for all the healers to be trained as midwives are, so our compassion, wisdom and expertise can aid the evolution of humanity and bring it to higher vibrations of Divine Love. Ancient and sacred healing practices, from a time before the material and spiritual were deemed separate, are being re-earthed.

It is an exciting time. While there is intense resistance in our midst, as patterns of limitation rise to the surface to be felt and acknowledged, allowing healing to occur organically, the potential for humanity to Awaken is greater than ever before.

We must come together and support each other, as we vacillate from facilitating expansion to birthing it. The healer is healed as she heals. The healed becomes the healer. When a woman gives birth, she is simultaneously the birther and the birthed. For, she has known the one within her body as an extension of her very own being. Literally, they were One as they became two. The Ultimate truth is that We Are ALL One. All energy is unified and vibrates at various speeds; yet, we all come from the One and merge back into the One, as the Great Creator breathes us in and out for eternity. As we understand this truth, a freedom and fearlessness will take hold in the consciousness of humanity, which will be deeply rooted in Oneness and Love. The eternity of Life and its inter-connectedness will be felt and known on a visceral level, beyond thought and mind.

This is my prayer.
This is my belief.
This is my choice.
This is my truth.
This is my knowing.

The one thing I know is that, while we cannot control many conditions in life, we do have a choice about what we believe and how we perceive. Cultivating conscious choice, conscious and deliberate focus, is the way to marry our desires to our manifestations. This is how the Law of Attraction works its miracles in a way that facilitates the most joyful and brilliant expressions of our desires. Regardless of our focus, however, I am confident that we will be guided to our expansion, and while some paths are more arduous and the resistance at times may feel unbearable, the journey is rich and varied, and expansion is assured.

36

Intimacy

W HAT DOES IT MEAN TO be intimate? The concept has been one that has eluded me for a long time. Am I afraid of intimacy? Am I really willing to be intimate? Am I holding back from life, from my lover, from my relationships? What scares me—being vulnerable, being hurt?

It seems to me that it takes courage to be intimate, and intimacy starts with the Self. Intimacy, when mastered, is the highest spiritual ideal, because it allows for a sweet, delicious connection to All That Is. It recoils from nothing. It walks into the darkness, the earthy barren fields of the unknown, and brings a living breathing expression of Love, which embraces the mystery as it steps into thin air, unafraid and unconcerned as to where its foot will land. Intimacy takes Faith—Faith beyond words. Faith that viscerally knows all is well, that I am safe, that I am One with all of life. Even that is too many words and inadequate to describe the Faith that Intimacy knows.

I yearn to be intimate—fearlessly and recklessly intimate—with all that shows up in my life.

Intimacy is an Open Heart, a spacious mind, a body that melts into the surrounding molecules of moisture, indiscernible to the senses, but utterly intoxicating to Intimacy. Intimacy risks vulnerability without a second thought, because it knows it is intrinsically safe and that, in truth, there are no risks. Intimacy embraces fear and transforms it into Love. It is alchemy. It is the eyes of the newborn, whose unflinching gaze takes you in, into the Love it is, without apology, explanation, requirements or neediness.

Intimacy is flawlessly free,
utterly and completely.
It requires intimacy to be Awake.
It transforms the mind and lives deep within the heart.
It is the surest and sweetest path
back to the Self.

37

Blessings in Disguise

BLESSINGS OFTEN COME IN DISGUISE. The disguise can be painful, emotionally or physically or both. This past month, I have been forced to deal with a physical condition that I have been struggling with on and off for eight years. It is still undiagnosed and has felt somewhat like an enigma, a mysterious bout of painful stabbing spasms just below my diaphragm. It would come, last for twelve to twenty-four hours, and life would go back to normal. Because I believe that all physical symptoms stem from emotional and mental blockages, I was determined to figure out what was happening to me on a vibrational level. I did experience relief from the pain for eight months after I started taking the Flower Essences, which I thought was a miracle. When the episodes of pain started to become regular again, I was disappointed and frustrated.

Apparently, my life was offering me an opportunity for expansion, through this blessing in disguise, when I was forced to deal with this condition that had been gnawing at me for too long. On August 30, 2015, during a painful episode, which persisted for more than ten days, I went to the emergency room and began the process of finding my path to healing.

I am in the process of this medical evaluation phase now. In the meantime, I continue my vibrational inquiry, which has led me to work with an Energy Healer Chrys Franks, who is a beautiful, powerful, wise and humble being, who uses the modalities of Reiki, Crystals and Akashic Records for her healing work.

Reiki is a healing technique based on the principle that the therapist can channel energy into the patient using touch to activate the natural healing processes of the patient's body to restore emotional and physical well-being. Crystals contain healing frequencies, much like the flower essences, and each stone offers different properties to heal and transform the vibrational body of the client.

The Akashic Records are essentially a vibrational record of the Soul's journey and offers a broad and spiritual perspective to support and guide one's present experience. It truly is a field of Infinite Possibility, Divine Intelligence and Unconditional Love. Therefore, it is profoundly healing simply by being in the 'Field,' but the main intention is to receive clear guidance offered by the Masters, Teachers and Loved Ones who give specific information that will be most helpful for you and your personal development at this particular time.

So this past week, I went to see Chrys, and what was revealed was the blessing beneath the pain. I sat in a chair, while she started the session by doing some Reiki on my head. I had told her my head was hurting when I first arrived. As she sent energy into my head and the base of my neck, I felt this cool sensation drape across the top of my head and over my face. The headache was instantaneously gone! I have never felt anything like it! It was so immediate. She shared that, for her, it felt like a bubble bursting right at the base of my neck. As the session continued, I was aware of fluctuations in energy and inner shifts and releases throughout my physical and emotional body. While she was being guided from within my Akashic Records, my Masters asked me to find the memory that was connected to the fear I had been feeling in my body. At first, I was unable to find one. Nothing came to me. Later in the session, they asked me again to see if I could find the memory.

I closed my eyes and took some deep breaths. An image of my father, leaning with his arm outstretched against the refrigerator, came into my mind. My mother was to the right of him, and I was sitting at the kitchen booth across from them. I was little, only seven years old, and I was looking up at them as they told us children that they were separating, and Mom was moving out.

At this point, a flood of tears poured out of me. I was a bit surprised, because it was a scene that I had not thought of in ages, and I honestly thought I had already resolved my feelings about this pivotal moment in my life. I told Chrys that at that time, I had thought I was going to be an orphan. I remember my parents explaining to me that they would both still be our parents, and we would still see them both. However, in my seven-year-old mind, I was at a loss. I did not understand what was happening, and I was terrified. My world, as I knew it, was crumbling all around me. I remember feeling as though my life came into sharp focus after that day. Everything before that day became a dreamy, filtered haze, and my memory of my early childhood receded into oblivion.

Chrys emphasized that this was an important event, and the little me had become frozen in fear at that moment. She never evolved but stayed stored in my cells for all this time, and whenever fear arose in me about a current situation, she would be activated along with the fear that makes her ask, "What is going to happen to me?" With my recent physical challenges, her fear has been more active than usual. She also said that was the moment my voice was shut down. I did not have a say. Not only did I shut down my voice, but I also slowly closed my heart, over the following years, to protect it from breaking. Over the past couple of months, I have been aware of a tight sensation in the front of my neck and throat. It feels like fear is stored there, and now I am aware, as fear arises, that I sense it either in my throat or in my gut, where the pain radiates from the spasms in my diaphragm.

The Masters recommended that I pull her into me and be willing to have fear in my experience, to feel the fear. In a way, I haven't allowed myself to feel the fear, especially the old, past fear. I have been trying to find a way not to feel the fear, to be healed from it. I have felt hindered by the fear and frustrated by it. wishing it away, believing that it has held me back and paralyzed me at times, particularly when it came to public speaking. It made me shy. It was exhausting to run from this fear, and now I realize I have been running from this scared, stunned seven-year-old. I left her there on that fated day, and as part of me evolved, this other part stayed behind. I did the best I could. Shutting down and shutting her out was a coping mechanism that the seven-year-old mind subconsciously invented to deal with the uncontrollable condition. Now, forty-two years later, I have the opportunity to integrate this part of me back into my life, so that I can become whole. I must be willing to have fear in my experience, to feel the fear and not try to fix it or heal it. Feeling the hard emotions that arise are all that is required for them to let go of us. Suppressing the feelings is what gets us in a load of trouble. They get stored in our cells and eventually wreak havoc on our lives and bodies.

I am so grateful for the awareness and the opportunity to feel the fear I never fully felt, so I may reunite with this part of myself and become whole again. I am excited about the possibilities of having this access to this young self and the first seven years of my development, which is a precious and crucial part of my Being. I am grateful to be able to soothe, comfort and love this child within me that has been alone and scared for too long. I am strong, powerful, loving and connected to Divine Guidance and can offer all of this to her, so she can evolve and grow into the fullness of what we have become. I look forward to integrating and remembering the precious gifts of her seven years prior to this day, that were based on informative early years that were carefree, child-like, safe and loving.

It has been four days since this healing session, and I have written my little 'Becky' a long letter asking her forgiveness, loving her and letting her know what a wonderful life we have and to share the evolution of it with her, assuring her that everything turned out well. I have found a couple of pictures that look like I am about that age, and I am drawing her a picture that I know she would love. She loved to draw more than anything, with her huge set of markers of one hundred or so colors, at the table her grandpa made for her and her sisters. I have sent love and energy to the event that froze her in time and wrought her with fear. I envisioned myself at that age speaking up, crying and yelling at my parents for making such a horrible choice, telling my dad to get on his knees and beg my mom to stay and fight for her—screaming at her for leaving. How dare she? How could she? The loud, strong voice of a seven-year-old. I am helping her now to have a voice, a voice she couldn't seem to conjure that day.

As I was in meditation, I decided that I would call my mom and go over to let the seven-year-old speak to her mother herself. I let Mom know what I was doing and what had occurred in my session with Chrys and asked her if it was okay. Of course, she said yes. I cried and spoke strongly, and she listened. It was not important what Mom said at this point. All I needed was the opportunity to speak up and for her to listen. The little me is my responsibility now. I wanted her to have her voice and give her the opportunity to feel the anger that she never felt safe enough to express. I asked my mom to share some memories of me in the beginning years. It took her a moment to remember, but she found some memories of the kind of person I was. She said I was happy and carefree. I was not overly concerned about others, which I consider to be a healthy childlike behavior, which I lost after that day. Even if it didn't seem like it from the outside, I was so worried about other people and their well-being that it became a burden on me that *no* child should bear. It was a coping mechanism. I assumed I would be okay, if everyone else was okay. It is a pattern that I have only recently begun to unravel. It is the very source of my addictive pattern of thought, which I have been investigating through my work with the 12 Steps.

I had identified my addiction as the addiction to the well-being of my oldest son, and now I realize that it was much more pervasive than that. It was the addiction to the well-being of everyone around me. As long as everyone around me is well, especially those I love, then I will be well. If I can control, not only my world, but also the world of others, then I will be safe and loved. Wow! Hopeless. A lost cause. Yet, I attempted to control this in my mind, by taking care of others emotionally and feeling responsible for their happiness. I have been aware of some of this patterning, and I have consciously worked on it, and yet, this feels like a new crucial part of the puzzle. Its origins feel clear now; therefore, I am sensing this incredible potential to release it, to heal it and integrate its purpose. I feel like I now understand. The little girl, who grew up instantaneously, left childish things behind. I abandoned the little girl to avoid feeling her fear.

I think this is the case for so many of us. I am certainly not the first to be 'robbed of her childhood,' and certainly this kind of disassociation happens every day, as the myriad of life's conditions, far worse than the divorce of your beloved parents, can traumatize little people. It can be smaller events than this as well that can create a shift, a trauma, a new perception or a splitting from yourself which determines a whole new path towards your own particular expansion.

There is nothing about my past that I would want to change. I made peace with it a long time ago, and I appreciate the benefits of not having my parents stay together for various reasons. I would not have lived in the Bahamas for my high school years, nor would I have been exposed to a whole new and unique perspective of art that greatly informed my creative process. I love the relationship that I have shared with my mother over all these years, which has been a deeply spiritual path of self-investigation and exploration of the Divine dimension of life. Her path, which included leaving her marriage with my father, has not been an easy one, but it has been authentic. Following her inner guidance, which was far from popular at times, modeled for my siblings and me what it means to be true to yourself.

My father remarried a woman who has offered another dimension of richness, growth and love into my life, and their union brought forth my beloved sister, Mary Beth, a connection for which I am very grateful. This intense contraction, which this early experience in life brought, was the birth of the life that I have lived and loved. It has been one of expansion, creativity, spiritual awareness, compassion and deep longing for harmony and peace, as well as passion and purpose.

I am grateful to now have the opportunity to reintegrate, heal, love and, most poignantly, to acknowledge and *feel* this part of myself, which I unwittingly abandoned, as I ran from my fear on that fateful day forty-two years ago. The process of evolution and awakening is never-ending.

This story of this moment continues to unravel, and I am sinking into the process, not knowing what will come next, but I am open, more now than ever, to accept each moment as it arises, with less and less fear; yet, I am willing to have fear in my experience. I will not run from it nor stuff it into the cells of this precious body anymore. I will face it, feel it and allow it to let go of me when it is ready.

This is the time to practice Unconditional Love. Regardless of the condition, I will practice staying aligned with Love—love that, in the face of fear, is intimate and transformative—love that embraces all of life as it shows up—love that stays fearlessly present, even when we choose to remove our body from a toxic situation—love that dares to be intimate with that which we deem unlovable.

38

Waiting

HAD A BLOOD TEST YESTERDAY that would indicate the possibility of whether I have cancer or not. I went to the lab by myself, even though I have a history of passing out when having blood drawn. I decided I did not need Sherman to come with me, because I wanted to feel like my strong grown-up self. I wasn't sure if I would be told the result right then and there, so it felt pretty courageous for me to do this alone. I was proud of myself. I stayed optimistic, aligned in joy and smiled genuinely to each lovely person I met along the way. I made it through the blood draw with ease and maintained a feeling of joy within me for the rest of the day.

Today, I discovered that I will not find out the result for several more days. I am not feeling as fortified today. Fear has been washing over me in waves, and thoughts of the potential outcome of the dreaded disease keep nagging at me. I recently learned the word 'fabulism' at a teacher's education night at my son's school. They described it as a condition that afflicts adolescents, making them feel that bad things can't happen to them. Well, I never really outgrew that fabulist perception. I really do not believe this can happen to me, and while I still don't know what the prognosis is, I am feeling vulnerable at the mere suggestion.

I have a 'lesion' on my right ovary. I am getting additional tests, unrelated to this ovary situation to attempt to find out why I have had, and continue to have, intermittent episodes of pain in my upper abdomen. What the hell! I want to know, and I don't want to know. I want to bury my head in the earth, cover my ears and sing as loud as I can to stay in the fable-land of yesterday. And yet, I want to expand and grow and break through old fear and emancipate my mind and heart *more* than living in a fable. I want to practice Unconditional Love and feel that Love that I am right now, regardless of the fear that is present at this moment. I want to be able to practice this Unconditional Love, no matter what shows up on the tests, and to be able to continue to tap into the joy that is my very essence. I want to be willing to move through the fire of this fear, no matter how much my chest burns, and fall into the metaphorical arms of Source. I want to have faith—faith in my well-being, a faith I struggled to have for my own son, as he fearlessly ran through the flames for his own baptism. I want to be free of this fear.

"Are you willing to die for your freedom?"

"But can't I be free in the body? Can't I be free while making love to my beloved? Can't I be free while I mother my children? Can't I be free while I am working to make money, while I create art, walk this earth, sing and dance? This is the freedom I want. I want to be free in the physical world. There is time for the freedom of being spirit. I want it here and now. Right now!"

"Then you must stay present.

Don't leave with your mind.

Your body needs you to be here now.

Your presence is required, if this is what you want.

You must sit in the intimate breath of this moment.

Simply breathe.

Freedom is now.

Notice the sensation of goosebumps tingling throughout your body,

the air moving into and through your lungs,

cooling your insides.

Feel the energy of life cascading over your body, and let your heart open,

slowly,

with each breath.

Freedom lies in Love

Unconditional.

No matter what the condition,

you are meant to be free.

Freedom is not controlling conditions or escaping them.

It is staying aligned with Love no matter what shows up!"

"Help! I feel so much fear around this condition. Possibly, it is my biggest fear.

Give me a sign, please. I could really use an indisputable sign. I am afraid for myself and my family. Why is life so hard?"

"You make it harder than it is. When you indulge in the thoughts that create the fear, you separate yourself from your Source. When the fear arises, watch it the way you might watch a thunderstorm. As you know the storm will end, so will the fear. Do not judge yourself for your fear. Simply observe and feel the sensations that arise in the body, without judgments. If judgment arises, observe those as well, and allow the light of your True being to be present as the observer.

Your sign will come to you with clarity. Now, wait, sweet child of the universe. Rest in the cocoon, and allow yourself to be wrapped tightly in the womb of creation, and have faith in your emergence, your blossoming, your flight."

39

JOY NOW

YESTERDAY, I WENT TO MY healer for energy work and more . . . so much more. My guides told me they want me to live with more JOY. They said that they want me to take the stance of curiosity and joy, and as the fearful thoughts or sensations arise, which honestly have been feeling more like being attacked, to notice them with curiosity. Instead of taking a fear-based perspective, where I create a story of a horrible future and wonder fearfully what will happen to me, she suggested that I ask myself these questions: "I wonder what will arise next? What opportunity is being offered? What is the gift in this experience?" She also suggested that I take the fearful thoughts and feelings and put them in a crystal ball, which I like, because I imagine the crystal as an energy transformer. She said that when the thought comes, to recognize it and notice if it is true, which most of them are not. Then, put it in the ball. We talked for a while and then she did Reiki energy work on me for some time. When we were done, I felt so much joy. I felt relief, and I felt supported by the Universe, through her work with me.

I began the practice right away, along with holding my attention on my body and breath, supporting me in becoming one with the Now. It is so powerful to be in the presence of Now. I could feel the tingles run through my body and the activation of divine connection.

This morning, I woke up feeling so much joy. The silent words running through my mind were, "I am so happy. I am so grateful. I am so blessed." I decided to go to a Nia class, a spirit-filled form of dance that I have not done in a long time. I felt excited about dancing in communion with others and giving this gift to my body and spirit. I drew an angel card from my deck before I left, quietly wishing it to be the card 'Singing and Dancing,' that I drew a couple of weeks before, after my session with Chrys. Blessedly, it *was* the card I drew! It felt like a true sign that my angels are with me every step of the way. Waves of goosebumps are constantly cascading over my body now.

I joyously danced and opened my heart to all the women in the class. I felt so present in my body and heart. When I got home, I received a call from my doctor. She sweetly and cautiously shared with me the results of the blood test from earlier in the week. The numbers were slightly escalated; therefore, it was considered positive, indicating a possibility of cancer on my ovary, but not conclusive by any means. She is referring me to an OBGYN oncologist, who will be able to obtain and offer more information.

So, the most awesome, amazing and magical thing is that I am still in a state of pure joy and gratitude! I am not gravitating back to the fearful thoughts. It has only been one day of practicing Joy and present moment meditation, and I am still holding this stance. I am in a state of Unconditional Love. I am willing to be in the pause, the waiting. At this very moment, I don't need to know what is happening in my body. I am in the awareness that my body is continually changing, and nothing is stagnant unless we perceive it that way. Whatever arises and reveals itself to me, as I investigate the inner world of my body, is just as it should be at this moment for my personal and spiritual evolution. The peristalsis of my life is not only necessary for the eventual birth and expansion of all that is desired, but it is also the process by which I expel and release all toxic energies that keep the natural process from flowing smoothly.

Contraction, expansion, contraction, expansion. . . .

Bathed in the energy of Divine grace, I feel full, brimming over, full of love and gratitude. My heart bows in humility to Life and the overflowing of Love pouring fourth from the Divine Realms. I am not alone, I never have been . . . ever! I am in love with life and everything contained within it. I am in the intimacy I described earlier, utterly and intimately awake to Now, sweet surrender to all that is, infinite joy, infinite peace, indescribable love, deep compassion, sinking in and becoming one with life. I am unattached to thoughts of future and past, allowing a delicious merging with the Divine Field within all things and the space in between.

It is such a paradox that the yogic practice of detachment brings us to the most intimate union with the essence of all of Life. We must hold lightly to that which is precious. To cling to it may suffocate us or cause us to stagnate. Like an egg within the ovaries of a woman, which holds the origins and imprint of life, life must be held lightly, or we risk cracking the shell in our clinging and fearing. To hold life lightly in this way, gives us the courage to risk just enough to live fully and gives us just enough reverence to keep it from falling to the ground.

What is to come next? What will my next expansion look like? What will the gift be? Will I be able to expand as big as my soul desires and remain within the tender shell of this body? Am I willing to hold Life lightly enough, so my shell won't crack? To what do I cling? To whom?

I contemplate curiously. I hold the questions lightly.

I sit on my screened-in back porch listening to and watching the hard, steady rains cleanse and nourish the earth and marvel at how the intention of the rain is simply to rain, because that is what it *is* and what it *does*, and inadvertently, its self-expression sustains life. The flora breathes out oxygen and breathes in the carbon dioxide we breathe out. We sustain each other. The symbiotic relationship between all intricate aspects of life is beyond our comprehension, and yet, it is undeniably incredible. Could it be that our very being is enough to nourish Life? Could it be that we are an intricate aspect of the Divine tapestry that allows all else to BE? Could it possibly be our essential and intrinsic purpose is simply to BE, and everything else is the joyful expression and expansion that occurs as a result of our Being? I wonder if possibly, for those of us who are not experiencing this intrinsic joy that is present in Life, or when we are not, that we have lost sight of our essential Selves and forgotten our pure and natural ability to BE.

To be fully here NOW is to BE living our highest purpose—all else is infinitely nourished from this simple vibrational stance.

40

Healing Journey to Wholeness

I T HAS BEEN ABOUT TWO months since I have written. I have been on a profound journey of healing and expansion through a portal of physical pain and emotional contractions. It has been a powerful journey of joy, gratitude, fear, resistance and expansion. I have learned so much about myself and the frozen aspects within me that have lived in the cells of my body as fear and pain. In a way, the last two months have been an epic adventure, as I have delved into my healing journey towards wholeness with unbridled desire from my Soul to evolve.

I feel reverent gratitude for the conditions that have emerged to offer me the impetus to expand beyond my comfort zones, which have kept me stagnant. I have yearned to shift and transform these stagnant areas but had no idea how to make that happen. My conscious, deliberate intention and focus, which I previously practiced, while powerful and useful in many cases, could not penetrate the pain and fear that was calcified in my body and mind. I do believe that my insatiable hunger for freedom and joy and fearlessness led me to the unexpected path that would begin to thaw the frozen aspects of my being, offering me the opportunity to experience my wholeness.

One of the ways in which I have consistently received Divine Guidance throughout my life, is to write in my journal in a dialogue format, where I ask God questions about how to deal with situations in my life. I have volumes of journals with beautiful and profound writings, channeled for my personal clarity and guidance. Eventually, the dialogue format shifted to the process of 'Opening my Akashic Records,' using a sacred prayer to enter into this Divine Field. When I began to do this, I realized that I had been both writing and painting from this Energy Field of Divine Guidance for most of my life. I just did not have the language or concept to help define what I was experiencing. Once I began 'receiving' within the Akashic Records intentionally, I felt the familiar resonance with it and recognized that this was 'home' for me.

During the time that I was deliberating about how to deal with my mysterious health dilemma, I consulted my Guidance in the Akashic Records. While writing, I asked my guides for direction. I was clearly offered the instruction to go to Chrys and to arrange to work with her on a regular basis, both for my own healing process and to learn from her for my personal and spiritual evolution in expanding my healing work, which I would be offering others. At this point, I was seeing clients to provide consultations with the Bach Flowers.

So, this is when I began my journey with Chrys, which has been invaluable. Her clear messages from my own Divine Guidance has ushered me toward a whole new trajectory in my life. Not only have I experienced profound healing and deep understanding of the nature of what arises in my body, mind, and heart, but also her mentorship has ushered me into a powerful Awakening of a new me, as a vibrational healer! She has guided me in how to work with others in their Akashic Records, and she initiated me into the healing work of Reiki. This painful, long, hard contraction has been an absolute blessing in disguise, giving birth to a whole new beautiful way of perceiving and receiving life for the expansion and evolution of myself and others.

I hoped, when I first began working with Chrys, that I would receive a definitive answer as to the cause of my pain. I was hoping for a diagnosis from the Divine. Sometimes Chrys will get a direct answer, but with me, my Guides did not offer this clarity but took a different approach that encouraged awareness about the deeper roots of my malaise, which was to be revealed and healed gently over time. In retrospect, I totally understand why this approach was offered. I surrendered to this process of unfolding and experienced the most delicious, profound healing, which awakened me more deeply to my whole Self and to a sweet freedom that continues to expand.

I was encouraged by my 'Masters' to get the medical tests done and to follow that process, while continuing to receive healing sessions with Chrys. So, this is what I did. The medical tests included ultrasounds, a colonoscopy, an endoscopy, X-rays, blood work and visits with specialists, none of which offered a clear explanation for my discomfort. It ruled out some things, but mostly it became a part of the mysterious process of healing the body and mind on a vibrational level. Of course there was also the blood test that revealed the possibility of ovarian cancer, which certainly raised concern.

However, between the time that I found out about the

lesion and the appointment with the oncologist, I had been going to Chrys weekly. In each session, I received the healing energy of Reiki, and we would work in the healing frequencies of the Akashic Records. I was unearthing memories that were living in my cells but not in my conscious awareness. I had significant releases and many epiphanies.

In the meantime, I intuitively decided to change my diet. While most people who know me would say I have a very healthy diet and have been very conscious about my food choices, I made some major changes. I stopped eating meat, except for seafood. I eliminated wheat and refined sugar from my diet, as well as alcohol. I knew that cancer feeds on sugar and did not want to wait to find out if that was what I had in order to begin to change what was going into my body. I drank smoothies most mornings with fruit and spinach and lots of beets. I took probiotics, and I studied about healing foods. I felt like I was in a detoxification period, and that it was necessary because I was extra sensitive on all levels at that time. I believe that I had support and guidance from the nonphysical realm of angels and guides to be able to change my habits and easily let go of these foods that I had been consuming every day. I became lighter, both physically and energetically. Little did I realize at the time that this vibrational shift in my body was part of my preparation to evolve as a healer.

As I continued my journey of healing and self-discovery with Chrys, one day I asked what step to take next, and the Masters very clearly stated that it was time to get my Attunement for Level One Reiki. Chrys asked, "When?" They said, "Now." As a Reiki master, Chrys is able to perform the ceremony that initiates one into the practice of Reiki. At the beginning of the Attunement, she called forth any beings of light that would like to be present during this ceremony to support and offer me guidance. She later shared with me the visions she had received during the ritual. I love hearing about what visions and information come to her during our sessions.

She shared that three beings came into the room and stood in front of me during the Attunement. First, she saw Archangel Jophiel, the angel of beauty. Then, the Goddess Isis emerged in regal garments, wading in water. She then described a male figure coming forward, whose energy was very relaxed and down to earth, and as he materialized, she recognized him as Jesus. Wow—how cool!

The energy of Jesus was most palpable for the days immediately after the session. I could feel lots of sensation through my body, letting me know he was with me as the miracle worker and healer. I felt as though my body was being healed, as tingles of energy cascaded over and through my body.

The very next day after the Reiki Attunement, I went to the appointment with the OBGYN oncologist. While I waited in the examination room for the doctor to arrive, which was about fifteen minutes, I could feel the energy of Jesus in the room with me. The atmosphere surrounding me was buzzing with this high vibration of Unconditional Love, and I felt an incredibly sweet sense of peace within me. I did not feel afraid or anxious at all about the impending prognosis of my condition. I knew that I was well! After all, I was in the presence of the Divine Healer, who performed miracles of healing, and so much more, during his time on earth.

When the doctor did the ultrasound, he could not find the lesion that was detected several weeks earlier, which prompted this whole investigation. He said that my ovaries looked normal for my age. He was not at all concerned and suggested I come back in four months for a recheck.

I was not surprised, because at that point, I felt the presence of the Divine so strongly that I knew that I was well, no matter what I felt in my body. I knew that I was healing and that it was more about healing my emotional, vibrational body which would have the most significant effect on my cellular physical body.

The process of healing and evolving and expanding continues, as I have received more opportunities to look at other remaining, painful, past scars, so that I may truly move forward on my path of spiritual expansion. I have come to realize that I have patterns of thought and behavior that are not so healthy and are directly connected to past trauma, and have been holding me back from my whole, Divine Self. I am not one to dig up the past in order to deal with issues that are no longer current. However, when the past arises in my awareness and reveals to me the way in which it is indeed still affecting my current experience, then I am grateful and willing to seize the opportunity to investigate it and grow from it, so I may live with more joy, love and freedom in my life.

The possibilities for expansion are endless, and the manifestations of Awakenings are infinite. As I continue to venture on this journey of lifting the veil to my whole Divine Self and of realizing my evolving potential, I trust each challenge that arises is present for my greatest good to unfold. I will even go so far as to say that my very Soul has brought me these creative opportunities to evolve. The less I resist, the more joy and magic I will feel, as I dance this dance required and requested of those who enter the realm of the physical.

And so, the journey continues, and I am grateful.

41

Vibrational Healing

EALING IS MUCH MORE THAN the restoration of
well-being within the physical body, although it is
the most common consideration when we think of
healing. My own process of seeking to heal my body from
recurring pain has revealed a vast and intricate landscape
of healing, which stems more from healing emotional pain,
caused by past trauma, small and large. The emotional issues
have become buried in a network of behaviors and patterns
of thought, which emerged as creative coping methods, as
I needed them. Of course, I did not realize it at the time, but
I was being creative, and I was learning coping strategies
to feel safe, as best as I could at such a young age. While
these strategies may have served me then, the continued
unconscious use of them throughout a lifetime has become
a problem. The feelings that I did not allow myself to feel,

became stored in the cellular structure of my body. When life circumstances trigger fear or loss of control, then the latent energy of old, unfelt fear is activated, and the past becomes the present, taking many undesired forms: fear of speaking my truth in public, physical pain and conditions, obsessive-compulsive behaviors that give the illusion of control, and emotional suffering. As Eckhart Tolle says, "The pain body is triggered."

I have always felt that it was important for all healing to be addressed from the emotional and vibrational body, as well as the physical level, particularly when dealing with more chronic conditions. This is why I am so drawn to the modality of Flower Therapy with the Bach Flower Essences, which work on the emotional and mental level. I do believe that if we treat the body exclusively, we can experience results that offer relief. However, I feel that, without the deeper work of healing the emotional, mental and spiritual bodies, the healing will often be superficial, and either the original problem will return, or a new condition will arise to inspire the opportunity for a more complete healing.

We all have our unique path to wellness and the options are infinite, and I do not wish to discount any approach anyone takes to feel better, to feel more ease, more joy or more freedom. Is this not what we all essentially desire? We are all on our own journey of healing, regardless of our levels of discomfort or dis-ease. I am considering the broader perspective, which sees the healing process as part of the human condition. It is about restoring our intrinsic connection to our True Divine Self and to the Infinite Love from which we all originate. In entering this world of polarity and illusive reality, which required us to forget our Oneness with the Divine, we experienced the pain of separation to different degrees. In our yearning to experience life and the great variety and diversity that this environment offers, we courageously plunged into this realm where we knew we would forget our wholeness, our brilliance, our Soul Self.

The process of healing, in this sense, is really the journey back home to the Ultimate Truth of our Oneness with the Divine. It is becoming *whole* again in the broadest definition of the word. Healing is restoring wholeness. To be whole is to be *all* of me. It is to embody the fullness of who I am as a Spirit, Soul and human being.

The healing modalities available to us are vast and diverse, spanning from simple organic approaches, such as using laughter, communing with nature, dancing, yoga, meditation, art, talk therapy, prayer, chanting, Reiki and healing touch, crystals, flower essences and aromatherapy to scientific approaches like homeopathy, chiropractic, naturopathic, acupuncture, network spinal analysis, nutrition, food healing and so on. Of course, there is the more allopathic, traditional approach, which focuses mostly on the physical body, with diagnostics, surgery and medications. The allopathic approach uses an array of therapies, which have been the most common in Western societies. All approaches have their place, and we each are challenged to find that which resonates with us most.

In my own healing journey, bringing balance to mind, body and soul, I have been guided and attracted to the modalities that primarily work on the energy body. The Bach Flower Essences, Reiki and the Akashic Records all tap into the higher frequencies that treat us on the vibrational level. It makes so much sense to me, considering that, according to Quantum Physics, 99.99999% of our bodies are energy at the subatomic level. It seems shortsighted to only focus on the .00001% of our body, as we attempt to heal. It is interesting how obsessed we have become with this small aspect of our being. Even science is now demonstrating how we are so much more than what meets the eye, particularly in the field of Quantum Physics. It is a fascinating time, as science and spirit are coming to an intersection.

As I have experienced the undeniable benefits of this approach, both personally and with others, I have become more and more excited about the possibilities for healing. Not only do I feel better in my body, but my life has also transformed in so many brilliant ways! I am now joyfully entering into a whole new and expanded expression of who I am in the world.

While working with Chrys, my healing journey evolved into a training process to develop more seriously my own work as a healer . . . the healer is healed so she can heal others. I had been given guidance on how to work with clients while in their Akashic Records to enhance the Flower Essence Therapy. I had begun to incorporate the Reiki healing into my sessions as well. The work was becoming richer and deeper, and I was trusting more and more in my own Inner Guidance and ability to channel what was offered to support the client in their journey to wholeness. Of course, I am not actually doing the healing. I am facilitating the process that creates an atmosphere where inner healing is optimal. This is the role of the vibrational healer. When I enter into the vibrational frequencies for healing, I am wholly aware of the intrinsic well-being of my client. I hold that knowing within me and allow the energy to flow through me to support the shifts needed for them to realize the Truth of who they really are.

I find it helpful to think of the physical symptoms that arise as a nudge to redirect or address patterns or conditions in our lives that do not serve us, or perhaps recognizing, like I have, the ways in which past patterns persist and hinder us from experiencing our full potential. Sometimes, the nudge is not heeded and becomes a tsunami, which will either take us out of this world or inspire us to embrace the transformation needed to truly heal, restoring our Divine connection with our Soul while we are still in our bodies. Reiki is a gentle process that gradually readies the person for the core-level healing that potentially restores balance on all levels.

Reiki and other healing modalities help us to release resistance. This releasing leads us to a more receptive mode for a shift to occur, which brings about the organic healing that the Soul desires for us. This may not lead to healing or to prolonging the life of the physical body, if the Soul is ready to leave this earth. Healing may be solely to promote a sincere acceptance of what is, which offers the true end to suffering. Suffering is the mind's resistance to what is. Pain is more bearable when we do not resist it with the thoughts and stories that torture us. We often think that healing is physical, yet I feel that the most profound healing starts in the heart and the mind, and usually the body will follow. Reiki healing is a beautiful exchange of the purest love and intention. Perhaps Love is the most powerful healer of all.

I am ceaselessly amazed and delighted by the genius and creativity of the Universe in offering ways for us to heal into our wholeness. On one fateful day, while in my Akashic Records with Chrys, I was instructed by my Masters to paint Soul Portraits for others, as a creative and sacred vehicle for healing and spiritual evolution. They suggested that I go into the Akashic Record of the client and channel their Soul onto canvas. The image would hold the frequency of their Divine Self, and it would contain symbols, colors, codes and energy patterns of light that would support the client in the process of embodying their Soul.

When we are able to truly embody our Soul, we not only heal on all levels from within, but we also experience life from the eyes of Oneness. We become Awakened. This is the most profound healing of all! Not only do we want to be healthy and vital, but we also want to be free, joyful and at peace. We want to feel our true power, to know our interconnectedness with all of life and to create consciously and deliberately our own reality. When we embody our Soul, we know we are One with All That Is; therefore, have access to the Source/Resource of the Universe. This Source is our essential Being and is what we call Love. To know this experientially changes everything! Abraham says that the basis of life is Freedom and the purpose of life is Joy. When we live from the Soul level, this potential becomes a reality.

Being offered this 'suggestion' to create Soul Portraits was the most brilliant expression of the Divine and Its Infinite intelligence. It is the perfect culmination of all that I have done to this point in my life, bringing together my art, spirituality and healing work in a way that is completely tailored to me and my unique offering. I was thrilled and dove in with fearless enthusiasm. I completely trusted that this was something I could do. While the healing work was relatively new to me, painting in this way was so utterly natural to me. I could not wait to get started.

My first assignment was to paint a Soul portrait of myself. It required me to go into my own Akashic Record and intentionally call forth my own Soul for this purpose. It was effortless and as familiar to me as breathing. This was when I realized that I have been painting from within my Akashic Records since I was seventeen! It started in my mom's kitchen studio when I painted *Silent Scream.* I was already aware that I had been writing from this Field of Energy, but I didn't know I had been painting from this place as well. As a matter of fact, *Silent Scream* was my first Soul Portrait. The wonderful thing is that when you live long enough to see the brilliant design of your life as a whole picture, you see the perfect order and symmetry of it all.

It is fascinating for me to see the symbolism revealed in the two paintings. The first Soul Portrait that I created at seventeen, was an expression of my Soul finding her 'voice' without sound and words, but with color, energy, light and movement. It has been a powerful voice imbued with the clear energy of my Soul. I channeled my second personal Soul Portrait onto canvas at age forty-nine, and this image reveals a serene, meditative face, eyes closed with an eight-pointed, star-shaped symbol at the throat area (or throat chakra), which is the energy center relating to communication. In the elongated neck there is a white shaft of light pointing down toward the heart, which brings your attention to the connection between heart and throat. The shoulders look like a collar of blue feathers, which for me, represent freedom and flight. The image has revealed its essential meaning to me and continues to offer its vibrational healing, particularly in liberating my voice and allowing me to speak from my heart with authenticity and confidence. What the flower essences started with healing my fear of public speaking, the Soul Portrait is taking to the next level. The transformation that has occurred as a result of this process is nothing short of miraculous. I am now speaking and sharing in public forums in ways I wouldn't have dreamed I would even have the desire to do, let alone think it was even possible!

When I began to paint Soul Portraits for others, being in their Records was distinctly different and wonderfully exciting. I am always curious and fascinated by what emerges onto the canvas. I love the process of creating these images for this very profound purpose of supporting the healing, transformation and evolution of the individual. I am deeply honored to do this sacred work, and I know without a doubt that it is a beautiful manifestation of my Life Purpose.

The process of healing is just that, a process, an unveiling, a revealing of many intricate, rich layers of the being in its Divine unfolding on the journey as a human Soul traveling through this adventure we call life on this magnificent planet we call home. The process of *healing* is not unlike that of *Awakening*. Awakening, too, is a process, an evolution, a revealing. Do we ever become healed or awakened, or is there a never-ending expansion that occurs in all realms of reality? I feel that we can become healed or awakened in a moment, and a blissful and sacred pause opens us up to the brilliant, ultimate Truth of our Oneness with the All That Is. This moment can feel like an eternity.

Then, we are offered the opportunity to continue on the adventure that promises to thrill and terrify us, as we plunge and rise through the magnificent and treacherous terrain of Life for the pure joy of expansion . . .

> *Expansion into the undeniable deliciousness of Love felt and expressed,*
>
> *hearts breaking, opening and soaring . . .*
>
> *Expansion into compassion that reaches deep into the heart of humanity . . .*
>
> *Expansion that creates beyond that which has ever been created before:*

art of all forms that delight and amaze,

the life of another, born into flesh to be loved and nurtured.

Expansion that allows us to touch the stars,

surpass all boundaries,

heal and Awaken

again and again and again.

42

Taking Flight

MY BELOVED FATHER HAS TAKEN flight.
He has left this earthly body, and has returned Home, to the origins of his Divine Self.

I wonder if the reason my book is not yet published, although on the verge, is because there is one last thing I am meant to add to it. Could it possibly be that I had one more Awakening to share with you before releasing this intimate, personal account of my Journey of Awakening? After all, what is more monumental in a person's life than the 'death' of a parent or of anyone very close to you? Using the powerful metaphor of birth throughout these pages, I realize I really had not spoken of the powerful alchemy that lies at the threshold of what we call death. But then, I had not yet experienced physical death so intimately.

This past year, I experienced the dying process of a dear friend, Reshuet. She had been a member of our Awakening group that met every Monday for four or so years. I had invited my friend Adaire to come to Charleston to do a talk at Utopia and lead an in-depth end-of-life workshop in my home. Adaire is an end-of-life doula and supports people as they navigate this profound transition in their lives. She educates us in how to proactively enter into the courageous conversation of death and helps us begin to make peace with this inevitable part of life, by offering us ways to prepare emotionally and practically. Because of this workshop, I feel Reshuet and all of us in the group were more prepared for the process of her transition. It was a very peaceful, beautiful home death, with those closest to her tending to her and loving her as she gently and without resistance released her body. While I felt waves of sadness, it was fleeting, and I seemed to be able to focus on the beauty of her transistion rather than the ache of loss that often consumes us. I think it is because she did not resist the process. She had very little pain without the need for strong painkillers. She felt at peace about where she was going, and she was not my dad.

A parent is someone we know our whole lives, and someone who knows us from the very beginning of our human self. Going to visit my dad the week before he took flight was so hard, brutally sad and utterly beautiful. I am so grateful that Nana called when his condition worsened and told me not to wait for when I had planned to go, which would have been two weeks later. I got on the plane the next day and had five tender, heart breaking, heart expanding days to be with Dad, as he moved closer to his exit from the body that I knew as my father for my fifty-one years on this planet. There is a lot of history there. With Reshuet, I met her as a mature, spiritually evolved adult within the format of diving deep into matters of Spirit, committed to removing the blocks to our freedom. We together understood the Divine nature of death as a powerful moment of re-emerging into the Infinite Self, the ultimate freedom. I felt the truth of it when Reshuet took flight.

So, I had no idea how I would handle the death of my Dad. Little Becky definitely felt threatened by this idea of her daddy dying. She felt overwhelmed with emotion, stemming from both love and loss. The evolved self was also present as we sat with Dad in his last days. I felt love and peace and so much gratitude. It was as overwhelming, if not more so, as the feeling of loss that little Becky was feeling. Mostly, I was in the driver's seat, soothing and comforting little B.

When we said our last goodbye, my whole self wailed. Love and loss sat side by side, and a river of tears released from my core, baptizing me with my father's love, his beauty, his legacy. I ached at the vision and sound of our last moments.

He was unable to speak that morning, mouth agape, but I could feel his embrace like never before. I heard a groan come from him as I pressed my cheek to his, lingering as long as possible. His groan seemed to express bliss and anguish all at once. The sweet intimacy of love and the deep ache of loss melded together in one last utterance. I kissed him all over his forehead and reminded him of our special word that he could use to send me signs of his presence from the other side. The word, 'cauliflower', seemed a strange and random choice I came up with one day as he ate cauliflower soup. He couldn't eat much those last days. As I was saying goodbye, I told him I like the word 'cauliflower', because it has the word 'flower' in it and it is a vegetable. He managed to get out a faint grin. His eyes barely open, I held his face and one last time told him I loved him. A million 'I love yous' over a lifetime. What a gift. So much love.

I rode the waves of intense emotion as I drove away form London, Ontario to the Detroit airport in Michigan, three hours away. By the grace of the Divine and Dad, I made it there in one piece. Each time a wave of achey heart-break welled up, I would receive a vision that I interpreted as Dad's Soul soothing me and watching over me along that journey home. Several times I saw white fairy-like seedlings flying abundantly through the air that I drove through. But the best was when I started to cry again, and I looked up in the sky ahead of me and saw cauliflower clouds. They had the distinct shape of a dozen or more cauliflower heads. I laughed at the sheer creativity of it! Who would have thought? I marveled at the perfection of my 'random' choice of words and thought how creative Dad could be in bringing me cauliflower signs.

The week that followed was tough for Dad, for the family that remained by his side and for those of us scattered like seeds in the United States. We were kept in the loop with updates and pictures. He had a few more good days as he rallied to receive visitors that offered their last goodbyes to this great man who touched so many lives with his kindness, humor and passion for social justice.

Then two days ago, as I sat with my mom and friend Bradley on Monday morning for our meeting, I opened my iPad to share with them a piece I had written about my dad. As I did, I saw that Nana was video-calling me on FaceTime. Of course my heart skipped a beat, thinking I was getting the news of my dad having made his transition. But no, he was still hanging in there . . . barely.

Nana brought the iPad over to Dad and put it close to him so that I could speak to him one last time. You see, the week after I left, it was just too hard for him to talk, so we let go of being able to be in verbal communication and I did not think I would get another chance. Again, grace. I was able to tell him it was okay to let go now, that we would all be okay, that I had been communicating with his Soul and that It was ready for him to reemerge with It and that there would be a great celebration of his homecoming. I told him that he had already sent me cauliflower, in the form of clouds, and that his soul was soothing me as I left him in Canada. I told him that I looked forward to the creative ways that we would communicate with each other once he was on the other side. He strained to respond with his open mouth, trying to turn his head and move his mouth with little to no avail. But I could see his valiant effort, and I could feel him taking in every word. Wow! It was such a gift that I had that last chance to say what I did, to see him right before he left his precious body, that was a shadow of the body I knew as my father. I am so grateful that my nana called, that my iPad was open for that moment, since it does not make any sound when I receive a video call on it. I was aware of the miracle of that! The magic of Divine Love orchestrated all of it. Perfectly. For each of us in our own way. There are many magical stories about these last days, and I know that there will be more to come as we all acclimate to Dad being out of body.

Within five or ten minutes after my last goodbye with Dad and talking briefly with Nana, I get a phone call. It is my sister Mary Beth letting me know that he has made his transition. Wow. The three siblings were simultaneously called by the siblings that were by his side, including Shawn, my brother-in-love, who was intimately partnering Nana through Dad's end of life transition.

Later that day, I was sitting on my back porch with Joanna, who was feeling utterly devastated. We were about to call our sister Sarah on FaceTime, and a striped tailed hawk swooped down into my backyard, landing on a low branch of a nearby hedge that both of us could see from where we sat. It was too heavy to be supported by the limb so it lifted off again revealing the beauty and majesty of its striped outstretched wings and tail. Magnificent! Undoubtedly, my Dad would not be limited to cauliflower. Later that evening, a friend came by the house with flowers and a tray of raw vegetables. Needless to say, the rainbow of veggies included a nice helping of creamy white cauliflower.

The day was wet and weepy in my house. Joanna stayed for hours. We began to make arrangements, to go back north for the memorial celebration, which honestly, gave me something to do that still focused on and honored my Dad. He consumes my thoughts, and even more so, I feel him acutely.

Yesterday, the day after he took flight, I woke up markedly clear and peaceful without any melancholy. I was a bit surprised. I felt Dad's magical presence all around me, and it made me feel joyous. I was eating my breakfast: cheese melted on a corn tortilla and sliced tomatoes with some fresh basil leaves. As I was gobbling it down to get ready for an appointment with a client that morning, I heard the words, "slow down". I felt Dad with me, wanting to relish the taste of my yummy little treat, something we ate growing up in Canada. He was with me enjoying the experience through me! I looked out my window into the big oak tree draped in Spanish moss framed by clear, blue sky, and it seemed more vivid and beautiful than ever. I felt waves of goosebumps, which are my indicator of tapping into the Divine. He is here—not out there! He is intimately connected to this world and to us, in a new way.

Somehow, I feel even closer to him now. I talk to him all the time and feel aware that I can call on him anytime. Just like those last moments when he could not utter a sound, I still felt him hear me intently. I knew he was receiving me and my words, my heart. And, I believe that he can hear me now. I have been practicing to sense, feel and know that which lies beyond what we see and hear. I have been cultivating my awareness of the nonphysical realm where my Dad now resides. With Dad in this new state, I now have even more reason to hone my awareness and receptivity to the Divine realm. I want to be able to receive him, as much as I desire that he hear me.

It is only two days since Dad's reemergence, but for now I am grateful to feel peace and joy and gratitude as my predominant emotions. I am open to all the emotions that emerge in me and look forward to feeling them as they arise. Sorrow is as delicious as joy, when felt spontaneously. Grief is welcome when it comes from the heart and not from the mind, because then it is born of Love instead of the anxious frequencies of fear, which robs us of the present moment. Love that cries is as welcome as the Love that laughs. Both nourish me and open me to the deeper truth and the Bare Beauty of this powerful lingering moment, when we sit at the feet of death and birth, birth and death.

The process of transition in both birthing and deathing can be painful and is always profound, but once the emergence occurs, there is a great and powerful sigh of relief and release. Both are a process, and the result of both is Life and Love Eternal!

43

I Paint

I am a Soul Artist and Vibrational Healer
that channels the Divine
to heal, connect and awaken.

I paint the bright, red, hot sun burning inside.
I paint
vulva, womb, women, mother, earth.
I paint germinating seed and blossoming bloom.
I paint bare beauty and naked intimacy.
I paint color
bold, wild, untamed and free
I paint sexy, sensual curves
and undulating lines.
I paint passion and peace,
Energy moving,
Vibration,
Soul,
Spirit.
I paint wisdom,

Bare Beauty

*the light
and the dark that it belongs to.
I paint joy unconditional
and love unbounded.
I paint heart
Broken. Wide. Open.*

*And when I open myself up to Divine Love,
It penetrates my heart,
revealing my Soul that is whole.*

*I reach deep into the dark void of infinite possibility,
squirt paint on pallet,
take brush in hand
and stroke fearlessly
COLOR
onto white nothingness*

*And I wait
with anticipation
and curiosity
to see what will emerge.*

*When I paint,
I surrender, allow
and connect
to the Infinite One and the Soul that I am.*

*I heal.
I am whole.
I am free,
And I. Am. Awake.*

44

Bliss

I BEGAN THIS BOOK WITH THE analogy of Birthing to describe the beautiful and brilliant design of the human experience and the living of life through 'painful' contracting conditions that offer the opportunity and propelling momentum toward expansion, the birthing of new life, a new creation. It was my intention and desire to honor the process as perfect and wholly whole—to give a perspective of this human experience that honors the varied paths and the vast range of emotions all as valid and necessary for the expansion and evolution of us All. I offered this metaphor to possibly soothe us all into this beautiful process of Awakening and Birthing our creations, as well as to encourage us to release resistance, so the unfolding that will eventually lead us all to this inevitable expansion might be a little or, hopefully, a lot less arduous.

I have come back to this simple and yet profound analogy

of birth, contraction and expansion as a way to understand this organic and natural process we are all experiencing within this human realm. It has been a very useful touchstone for me, as I continue this glorious journey of Awakening. I am Awakening more and more with each moment, feeling more and more into the nuances that gently prod me to my realignment with my Divine Self. While I am acutely aware of the emotions that are letting me know I am veering away from my Whole Self, I am more sensitive to the indicators, without needing the extreme, agonizing emotions to get my attention. Just a slight sense of off-ness can be too uncomfortable for me to ignore. I love, honor and am deeply grateful for the feelings that guide me. I am more quickly able to acknowledge them, feel them and release the limited thoughts that create them. I am fine-tuning my awareness and choosing the thoughts and perspectives that feel better, more and more often.

It is incredibly liberating and utterly exciting to recognize that I have a choice. I feel triumphant each time I watch myself choose the joyful perspective over the learned, habitual, limited perspective, which I may have unconsciously chosen in the past. I want to celebrate and tell the world, "I made a new choice today!" I choose bliss when, in the past, I chose pain under the guise of responsibility, remorse, validation, purpose, believing I am right, caring or even loving. I care more about how I feel than anything else, knowing that my feelings are leading me to my Awakened Self where Bliss resides, where God resides, where we are One. I choose freedom from any and all constructs, concepts and consciousness that holds me from my Bliss. I choose to live my life Awake—Awake to my inner guidance, so I can live Love without Condition. For when I feel out of alignment, I know I am believing that I need a condition to be different in order for me to feel Free, to be in a state of Love.

So, I choose Love above all else. When life presents its varied faces to me and asks me to respond, I will ask: "What would Love choose now? How would Love respond?"

All action will cease, and I will wait until the answer arises, no matter how long it takes. I will breathe deeply and sit with the trees and flowers and smell the sweetness of the air. I will feel the rippling waves of emotion that may be painful. I will stay with the undulating motion and elicit the embrace of the darkness, feeling the outstretching of roots wrapping me with ancient limbs within the lightless soil that sustains all life. I will ride the wave of the contraction with my breath and the awareness that I am held, I am safe, life is God and God is omnipresent. I will ask for the Love, that is God, for an answer, and I will wait as I writhe and relish in the dance and the labor that brings forth Love manifest, expanded and in the flesh.

I choose Love. I choose God. I choose Freedom. I choose Expansion and . . .

I choose to be Awake!

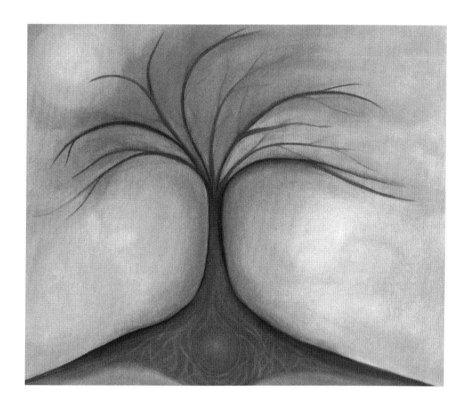

Afterward

absolutely love the way the Universe ceaselessly offers me opportunities to experience the expansion of Awakening. It is brilliant, beyond words! And yet, this last foray into Awakening has been all about words . . . words that penetrate the heart, into the spacious opening of clarity and awareness . . . words that deliver me to the essence of my own deepest truth.

I am in the last stages of completing this book. The delicious revealing of the content within this book came easily, effortlessly spilling out of me. It was the most organic, natural experience, not unlike the way in which I paint, sitting in the wonder and expectation of what will emerge onto the emptiness of white canvas. It has been a wonderful process of aligning with the Divine and allowing the words to come *through* me as much as they came *from* me.

Then, I had to consider the next stage of editing, publishing and all those practical details, and the process slowed down .

. . a lot. I did not quite know how to proceed, but Life continued to prepare me for this next phase, pulling me into the fertile soil where the seeds would germinate. During this time, some more blossoms arose to be added to the book, along with some profound healing around fears that might prevent me from truly 'baring my beauty' for all to see.

In this past week, I was inspired to change the name of my book. The name that I had come up with was solid and genuine, clearly expressing the essence of this book. Yet, one day I was talking to my mom when she casually said she was going to the movie *The Shape of Water*. As I absorbed the poetry of those words, I felt the desire emerge within me to have a title for my book that would take you beyond the mind and into the feeling and energy of the words. Poetry can often do that when it speaks to the heart and not the mind. My original title felt very literal. It was clear and strong, and yet it spoke more to the mind, rather than to the heart and soul. I wanted to *feel* my title . . . to be moved by it.

I delved into words and shared them with people I trusted, asking for their thoughts and opinions, but could not seem to get clarity. I wanted to feel certain; to hear angels sing and feel chills run down my spine. I asked my Divine Guidance why they were not handing me the title on a golden platter. Rather than a direct answer, I received encouragement to surrender to the creative process, which is really what this book is all about. Awakening is an evolving process *and* an experience that is happening in the moment—NOW. Awakening is endless, a journey that is expansive, filled with infinite possibilities. This process of writing and choosing the title has been an opportunity to dive into the yummy, sensuous world of infinite words and see what will emerge. Many words and titles began to reveal themselves to me. One title kept sticking.

It was not until I had a conversation with my friend Alex that clarity arose, as she expertly, gently, coaxed out of me what my attraction to *Bare Beauty* was. She had no preference or opinion, only questions, opening up a wide space for me to explore my inner knowing. "What does *Bare* mean to you?" she asked.

Bare speaks of emptiness, openness, unveiled, new life, naked and exposed. *Bare* is intimate, honest and humble. Yes, that felt true and true of this book. But it wasn't until I spoke out loud the word *Beauty*, that I felt my heart open, pierced with an overwhelming sense of wordless gratitude. I wept. How can I begin to describe what this word means to me?

Beauty

Beauty lays me out, bare naked, open, empty and full all at once.
Beauty is the experience of being human and divine.
It surrounds me and IS me.
Beauty embraces me and whispers to me
in the darkness when I am afraid.
It permeates all things and
wakes me up to the perfection of What Is.
I feel beauty in tears of joy and sorrow.
I know beauty in the eyes of my sons
and the first breath they took as they laid
bare naked
on my bare chest.
Beauty envelops me when I walk through wooded paths
with the ubiquitous color of growth surrounding me in all shades
of glorious green!
Beauty seeps into me as I ache desperately for the loss of a
dream or
a loved one.

Bare Beauty

Beauty enters me when I open to my lover, and we merge as one,
weeping in ecstasy.
I love the beauty of becoming,
forgetting to remember . . .
again and again.
Beauty inspires me with visions of color.
My God! Such magnificence is revealed through color . . .
the color of blood exposed to air,
the sky in all its glory,
the deep velvety brown of my baby boy's curls,
the aqua turquoise of the Bahamian sea,
the luscious rainbow of paint on pallet,
on canvas, vibrating with energy.
I am soothed by the beauty of silence and sound.
Awakened by the beauty of surrender,
soft and supple,
opening to the unknown
after a time of holding on for dear life.
I am breathlessly in awe when beauty dances sensual songs,
weaving the golden threads of humanity and spirit
into one grand masterpiece for all to behold.

When I am Awake, there is nothing that is not imbued with beauty.
Everything, at its very essence, is beautiful.

My Journey of Awakening reveals my Bare Beauty
and my Awakening to the Bare Beauty of All That Is.
May it inspire you to Awaken to the Bare Beauty in You!

Gratitude

offer my thanks to the Divine Source of Infinite Possibility and Unconditional Love that guided and inspired this unfolding expression of my life and the many Awakenings that have propelled my journey of expansion and evolution. For your enduring presence, guidance, comfort, prompting, love, brilliance, I bow with sacred gratitude.

The people in my life truly are a reflection and expression of the Infinite One expressed in Its utter genius and diversity, to support my journey in the most perfect ways:

My husband, partner in life and love, business and creation, Sherman Evans, has been my rock, my constant, my heart, my friend, always willing and ready to feed the sexy, sensual energy of Divine creativity in the way only he can. I am beyond grateful for his support in getting this creation to the next phase in layout, design and fruition.

My three sons, Chazaray, Noah and Kai each have offered their perfect and unique quality to support the evolution of my Soul. Mothering these brilliant, tender, wild, courageous, funny, intelligent beings has been the most fertile ground for the growth and blossoming that my wise Soul chose when I came forth in this physical body.

My mother, Elayna Shakur, has been an integral part of my spiritual evolution and more specifically, this book. She was the person that I knew I could send each chapter, as it emerged, to read and that she would offer the perfect non-judgmental and enthusiastic response that would give oxygen to the process of allowing the book to continue to reveal itself to me. As an astute and ravenous reader of spiritual material, she was able to fully receive the nature of my words and feel the fullness of their expression. It gave me a sense of being seen through the many months of receiving these words in silence and solitude.

My siblings all have both supported me and inspired me with their own unique creative expressions of the Divine in the form of words, performance poetry, dance and landscape design. Sarah, Joanna, Daniel, Mary Beth Crowell have each in some way, walked beside me in my creative and spiritual journey. For this thread of beauty and art that connects us, I am deeply grateful.

My Soul family, Alexandria, Adaire, Sarita, Bradley, Reshuet, Jeanne. Each have had a particular way of feeding my soul and midwifing me through my many labors, holding my hand, soothing me, supporting me and sometimes urging me on, reminding me when needed, that I can indeed give birth to this next brilliant expression of me.

My healer and Sensei, Chrystal Franks, who truly guided me in so many ways through this book, as she tapped into my own Divine Field of guidance while accessing my Akashic Record. Her guidance and healing has been invaluable to my eternal and creative process of Becoming.

My father and step mother, George and Donna Crowell, have always been a solid and supportive presence in my life that has allowed me to bloom in the way roots hold us to the ground, so that branching expansion and manifestation are sustainable. What a gift! Thank you for your rooted love and your commitment to family both blood and way beyond.

Life is full of awakenings, and the editing process was a 'sobering' awakening for me, when I realized the intricacies of perfecting a manuscript to bring it to print. All I can say is that it takes a village! Thank you to Cathleen O'Conner for the first edit that really got the ball rolling. Mary Beth Crowell, took it from there, offering her invaluable assistance in editing with the care and love of a sister who knows the truth of which I speak. I am grateful for all the eyes that miraculously found missed errors along the way. Of course perfection is the goal. However, I surrender and humbly release this work of art as imperfectly perfect, a true reflection of Life, and the one life I share with you in this book.

Simran Singh and Cassie Premo-Steele, for your kind words that grace the back of this book and the unique ways in which you each share your Bare Beauty with the world.

Tamra Scott, at the eleventh hour, offered the gift of her genius to create a book cover design that truly reflects the essence of my book and my journey of Awakening.

I am grateful for all those who have been a part of the branching possibilities to bring this book closer to its manifestation. For all those who have participated in small and big ways in my evolution and awakenings that make up this book and my life, I am deeply grateful. All are crucial to the Whole, the whole of me and the Whole of All That Is. Know that my gratitude for you reaches deep and wide beyond words and is held in the Heart of collective memory.

Bare Beauty

Inspiration

Byron Katie's books have been transformational for me and many I know: Go to www.thework.com to get familiar with her work. Favorite books: *Loving What Is, A Thousand Names for Joy,* and her most recent book , *A Mind at Home with Itself.* I absolutely love them all.

Eckart Tolle: *The Power of Now* and *New Earth.* Truly powerful and Awakening material that can change your life! www.eckarttolle. com

The teachings of Abraham: www.Abraham-Hicks.com I love anything from Abraham. You can listen to audio materials and videos on YouTube and they have a plethora of books, CDs, DVDs. A few of the books that I loved: *The Astonishing Power of Emotions, The Law of Attraction, Ask and It Is Given, Getting into the Vortex.*

Conversations with God books, by Neale Donald Walsch. All of them! Be sure to read *Home with God* , if you are interested in knowing what happens when we die. It offers some of the best material I have read about death and the afterlife. Books 1, 2 and 3 are a must. www.nealedonaldwalsch.com

The Prophet, by Khalil Gibran is a true classic, that offers timeless wisdom that nourishes and enlightens with the Bare Beauty of poetic prose.

The Parent's Tao Te Ching: A New Interpretation, Ancient Advice for Modern Parents, by William Martin. This book was invaluable to me as a parent and soothed me repeatedly as I flailed and floundered through parenthood. It provided the kind of advice that deeply resonated with my Soul. It is so simple and yet absolutely brilliant.

You are the Placebo by Dr. Joe Dispenza. More recently I have read his books which help to really make the connection between spirituality and science. He reveals the mysteries of the placebo effect and how we can heal our lives and bodies by using intentional thought and meditation. *Breaking the Habit of Being Yourself* is another wonderful book as well. He has all kinds of materials available to explore this approach and support your journey of healing and evolution. Go to his website: www.drjoedispenza.com

Charles Eisenstien: *The More Beautiful World Our Hearts Know Is Possible.* This book is a brilliant, beautiful and courageous exploration of the 'Story of Separation' that human culture is steeped in and how to begin to perceive more from the consciousness of Interconnectedness and Oneness. www.charleseisenstien.net

Simran SIngh: is a beautiful visionary and enlightened soul that offers a unique way of shifting consciousness with her words spoken and written. She transmits an energy, that dances on the wings of her poetic expressions, that is truly profound, that gently and unassumingly awakens the heart and mind. She has authored several books with more to come. www.iamsimran.com

Sera Beak: *Red, Hot and Holy* and *Redvelations.* She speaks the language of my Soul and is willing to bravely Bare her Beauty regardless of what others may think, and in spite of her own fear that arises. She is committed to diving deep and revealing her *real.* I am inspired.

i ate a rainbow for breakfast: poems and performances by Joanna Crowell. Brilliant, beautiful, raw and real, my sister shares her story and our story in prose in the most compelling and eloquent way. If you have an opportunity to experience her perform her poetry, you will be blown away. One minute you will be laughing out loud, the next you will be moved to tears.

Love Letters from the Divine Feminine by Mary Elizabeth Crowell. Deeply spiritual, simple and yet so profound, this gem of a book is a beautilful expression of the Love of Mother Mary received by my intuitive and sensitive sister, in the form of love letters. Timeless wisdom.

In my twenties, most of my reading time was consumed by the beauty and artistic genius of African-American women authors. Alice Walker, Toni Morrison and Maya Angelou were on the top of my list. I loved all their books. The story-telling, metaphor, realness and bold brave expression opened me to my love of literature.

There are countless more that I could include. The resources of Love's Inspiration are endless and are revealed through so many vehicles. For all the Beauty I have read, listened to, watched, and encountered throughout my life, I am deeply grateful!

Bare Beauty

ABOUT the AUTHOR

Beki is the Soul Artist and visionary of Utopia, boutique and gallery, in Charleston, SC, which she and her husband, Sherman Evans, have owned since 1991. She has been creating art that comes from, and speaks to the Soul for over thirty years. She has exhibited her artwork internationally and has especially enjoyed collaborating with other artists to create multi-media performance pieces.

As a reflection and expression of her own journey of Awakening, Beki now supports others to Awaken to the Bare Beauty within themselves. She blends the powerful and healing frequencies of Flower Essences, Reiki, the Akashic Field and her Soul Art to facilitate this Awakening. One of her most unique offerings is channeling the Soul of her client in the form of a Soul Portrait, which offers a profound tool for alignment, embodiment, healing and Awakening to the Divine Self.

www.bekiart.com

Made in the USA
Columbia, SC
11 September 2018